EGOLESS

THE FINAL FRONTIER IN LEADERSHIP

Dr. Sarah A. Morris

authorHOUSE®

AuthorHouse™
1663 Liberty Drive
Bloomington, IN 47403
www.authorhouse.com
Phone: 1-800-839-8640

First published by AuthorHouse   12/09/2011

ISBN: 978-1-4567-9820-8 (sc)
ISBN: 978-1-4567-9821-5 (ebk)

Contents

*Dedicated to all those leaders who dare to venture
beyond the realms of the known.*

Yet there are always a few who are not content to spend their lives indoors. Simply knowing that there is something unknown beyond their reach makes them acutely restless. They have to see what lies outside – if only, as Mallory said of Everest, "Because it's there."

This is true of adventurers of every kind, but especially of those who seek to explore not mountains or jungles, but consciousness itself: whose real drive, we might say, is not so much to know the unknown as to know the knower. Such men and women can be found at every age and in every culture. Whilst the rest of us stay put, they quietly slip out to see what lies beyond.

Then, so far as we can tell, they disappear. We have no idea where they have gone: we can't even imagine. But every now and then, like friends who have run off to some exotic land, they send back reports: breathless messages describing fantastic adventures, rambling letters about a world beyond ordinary experience, urgent telegrams begging us to come and see. "Look at this view! Isn't it breathtaking? Wish you could see this. Wish you were here." '

The Upanishads – Eknath Easwaran

Introduction

Over the past ten years I have observed first hand the obstacles, challenges and frustrations faced by today's leaders. I have seen what helps the majority of us at least partly overcome these obstacles and become adequate leaders. I have also seen some people emerge as exceptional leaders; although these are a rarer breed.

Exceptional leaders are transformational leaders. They are able to bring about a completely different level of performance in individuals, teams and organisations. They inspire trust and confidence and build sustainable working environments; and they are uniquely able to rise to the challenges we face, whether on a global, organisational or local basis.

We should not underestimate these challenges. If we cannot find a way of meeting them head on, it seems to me we face a pretty bleak future. Work is likely to become a place of increasing isolation, pressure and alienation where employees are more suspicious of their leaders and the organisations of which they are part; customers will continue the trend of becoming increasingly cynical about the corporations they rely on for goods and services; and our trust in governments and global organisations will remain low.

Many of us occupy leadership or management roles. We may enjoy the status the title brings and deliver acceptable results. Projects may be delivered on time and on budget and the teams we lead, whether large or small, may fulfil their roles adequately. But if we scratch the surface, and think more deeply about the way we lead and the results we achieve, both for ourselves and for those we lead, most of us cannot help but feel that there is something missing.

We are managers, yes; but are we truly leaders? Do we genuinely inspire those we lead and engender trust and loyalty? Are those we lead using their full potential and developing the skills and experience they need to flourish? Are we fulfilling our own potential and enjoying our roles and do we inspire real confidence in our followers?

Too often the honest answer to these questions is no. We may be adequate administrators but we instinctively feel there is something wanting in terms of true leadership. We know there is an alternative. If we are lucky, we may have seen it, having worked with a transformational leader or seen one in action at one time or another. What is harder for most of us to grasp is how we too can step out of our current mindset and behaviour patterns and become exceptional leaders.

For many of us, these exceptional leaders simply have an elusive quality we find hard to pinpoint or explain; that extra ingredient or inherent quality they are lucky enough to possess but eludes the rest of us. We would like to be like them, but get no further than that. But I believe there are clear distinctions between the behaviours and attitudes of those transformational leaders able to bring about a totally different level of performance and other more run of the mill managers.

The key distinction is ego. In my experience, ego is the single most important factor constraining leadership. Ego-full leadership is geared towards self survival and relies on negative behaviours such as control, manipulation, risk aversion and blame. Ultimately it hinders performance at an organisational as well as at an individual level.

Ego-less leadership, on the other hand, brings clarity, empathy and authenticity and creates balanced, sustainable and high performing environments; and it is this ego-less quality that actually defines transformational leaders. To fully realise our own potential, and to help those we lead to do the same, we need to find a way of moving from ego-full toward ego-less leadership.

Conscious Leadership is my vision for a new level of transformational, ego-less leadership, uniquely equipped to deliver exceptional levels of trust, sustainable working environments and more profitable organisations better able to meet their customers' expectations.

Here I set out a step by step guide to effecting this transition and emerging as a leader able to make the move from 'me' to 'we'. It takes readers through four key stages of transformation, beginning with the move from 'dysfunctional' to 'functional' ego, to authentic leadership and, finally, as we become increasingly confident and free of fear, ego is gently set aside and the *Conscious Leader* emerges. It is a profound journey and one which requires honesty, application and perseverance; but for those with the patience and humility to put in the time, and with a passion for becoming the very best leader they can, the results are well worth the investment.

Part One

The Case for Change

The failure of leadership

The challenges we face as leaders have never been greater than they are today. Across all sectors and countries, it seems the world of work is becoming ever more complex and ever more demanding; and whilst many of us spend a significant proportion of our careers aspiring to leadership, when we get there, the pressures and demands we face can leave the achievement feeling somewhat hollow.

Despite the material rewards leadership brings, other rewards can seem relatively thin on the ground, not least because so many of us do not feel fully equipped to rise to the challenges we face on a daily and hourly basis. Fewer than 40 per cent of today's leaders consider their development effective, and this is supported by the view of those responsible for their recruitment and development. Globally, only 18 per cent of Human Resources professionals believe the organisations they work for have the leadership strength to meet future challenges (source: DDI's *6th Global Leadership Forecast survey*).

We know there are some truly transformational leaders who do rise to the challenge and inspire individuals and deliver excellent results; but most of us feel we deliver acceptable results and there should and could be a better way of leading.

Challenges

Technological and other advances have made many aspects of working life easier. Processes that once took days now take minutes. Huge advances in communication allow us to email, call or conference with people all over the world at the touch of button and we can contact more people more easily and reach vast numbers of people within seconds, thanks to social networking and other tools. The internet gives us easy access to more information than we have ever had at our disposal before. Employers, service providers and others invest more and more in engaging staff and customers.

All should be well; and yet we feel mounting pressure, isolation and cynicism. All too often trust has broken down and we feel increasingly threatened by the environments in which we work and the colleagues with whom we work. We crave fulfilment and balance but our expectations are constantly dashed as work invades our evenings, weekends and even our holidays. Employers, on the other hand, are frustrated by skills shortages and scarcity of talent and employees who do not yet seem to have managed to get out of first gear.

> *Ever more people today have the means to live but no meaning to live for.*
> Viktor E Frankl

This is not a sustainable situation, and as managers and leaders we must accept our share of the blame. It is a failure of leadership that has led to too many employees feeling increasingly overwhelmed and impotent in the face of mounting pressure in the workplace, and that has contributed to the feelings of isolation and insecurity too many of us associate with work. As leaders, now is the time to take responsibility for putting things right; we must rise to the challenges we face and find better ways of working in the future.

> *It is a failure of leadership that has led to too many employees feeling increasingly overwhelmed and impotent in the face of mounting pressure in the workplace, and that has contributed to the feelings of isolation and insecurity too many of us associate with work… We must accept our responsibility to rise to the challenges we face and find better ways of working in the future.*

Expectation

Employees' expectations of work are higher than ever. We seek greater meaning from our careers and expect greater rewards, and this is particularly true of newer generations of employees. Work life balance is cited by employees of all ages and in all sectors as a critical, if elusive, factor in career and job choice and a greater proportion of the workforce looks to flexible working as a means of achieving the right balance for them. Employers are encouraged to accommodate new and more flexible ways of working and to consider employees' general rather than purely financial wellbeing.

> *Work life balance is cited by employees of all ages and in all sectors as a critical, if elusive, factor in career and job choice.*

There are countless examples of work life balance policies and practice benefiting employer as well as employee. Sickness absence rates fall, recruitment and retention rates improve, staff are more motivated and perform better and overheads fall. It seems shocking, therefore, that this is one area where so many of us feel very badly let down by the organisations for which we work and by our leaders and managers.

Engagement

Despite the increasing recognition of the importance of employee engagement and increasing investment in communicating with staff, all too often employees feel alienated from the organisations that employ them. Employee engagement rates are poor across all sectors and in organisations of all sizes; but they are particularly low amongst the young, with a new generation of employees feeling less engaged than ever.

We know the facts; engaged employees are informed about what is happening in the organisation they work for, are committed to that organisation and to its values and goals and believe their managers are too. They are given the opportunity to contribute ideas and to be involved in decision making; and they feel enabled to perform well and develop their role and because they feel valued, they contribute more to the organisation of which they are part.

> *Leaders consistently fall short when it comes to creating and promoting working environments where individuals and teams are valued, involved and able to flourish.*

Allowing these worrying trends of disengagement to continue makes no sense whatsoever. It squanders talent and opportunity and has an economic as well as human cost; and yet despite all the evidence supporting employee engagement, leaders consistently fall short when it comes to creating and promoting working environments where individuals and teams are valued, involved and able to flourish.

Trust

Perhaps the most shocking embodiment of the disengagement we feel from employers, organisations and colleagues is the breakdown in trust. We are not only cynical about governments and global institutions but also suspicious of our employers, managers and colleagues. Fear is creeping into many aspects of our working lives and this is hugely detrimental to our performance and mental and physical health.

> *Fear is creeping into many aspects of our working lives and this is hugely detrimental to our performance and mental and physical health.*

Far too many employees report being under excessive pressure at work and while many have a level of trust in their immediate line managers, they feel totally alienated from and undervalued by senior management. Even more worryingly, reports of conflict and bullying and work induced sickness and stress are commonplace. One in four employees report being subject to bullying and 42 per cent of managers say they themselves have suffered bullying (sources: Mercer Human Resources Consulting and CMI). Add to this day to day fears of being exposed as not being up to the task in hand, of saying the wrong thing, being reprimanded or complained about and we can see how lonely the workplace can feel.

Fear has other by-products. It stifles creativity, ingenuity and risk taking. If we are fearful of doing the wrong thing, we are necessarily also fearful of change; and without change there can be no progress. Fear breeds inaction, protects mediocrity and limits achievement. Ironically, it is often the very pressure organisations and leaders place on employees as they strive for ever better results and profits that cause the culture of fear that is actually the biggest barrier to achieving the excellence they pursue.

Falling short

Poorly performing, disengaged and disillusioned workforces that do not fully understand or embrace the aims and values of the organisations for which they work will never deliver the best results or profits. Nor will employees who feel overly pressured or bullied, alienated or ignored. But in far too many offices and organisations, this is the norm.

That the situation has developed in the first place points to a collective failure of leadership. Too many leaders blindly believe they are communicating vision, inspiring team members and building relationships based on trust and respect; but all the evidence proves this is simply not true. As leaders we have not only allowed this sorry state of affairs to evolve, we have been responsible for fostering the environments and cultures in which it has thrived. It is now our responsibility to put things right.

Transformation

It is a simple fact that we cannot solve a problem from the same perspectives and mindsets that created it in the first place; and to solve the problems we face as leaders and create inspired, productive and profitable teams of fully engaged and fulfilled employees, we need a radical shift in thinking.

> *You cannot solve a problem from the same level of consciousness that created it.*
> Albert Einstein

We know truly inspirational and visionary leaders do exist. Many of us know of them or are aware of people who seem to have the magic touch when it comes to inspiring loyalty and fostering excellence. This special breed of exceptional leaders are transformational leaders, truly able to bring about incredible shifts in performance, but what are the characteristics and behaviours associated with exceptional leadership?

There are many attributes that characterise these exceptional leaders. They are fair, empathetic, inspiring, and loyal. They recognise and reward the abilities and achievements of others and value creativity and risk taking. They are quick to share success and slow to apportion blame. They are driven by a 'we' rather than 'me' perspective, concerning themselves with the greater good rather than purely selfish and self-rewarding motives; and the single thing that most defines these exceptional leaders is their lack of ego.

I believe exceptional leaders are able to deliver results, solve problems and engender trust, and that they lead from an ego-less perspective. As a result, they are more resilient, better at engaging followers and they build stronger relationships; and, ultimately they deliver stronger performance and greater profits.

The *Conscious Leadership* model examines the attributes, characteristics and perspectives of ego-less leadership and sets out clear steps on the journey towards becoming a truly transformational leader able to engage, inspire and deliver exceptional outcomes.

Ego: the invisible saboteur

Ego is one of the most destructive forces at play in the modern workplace. It places significant constraints on leadership and has a negative impact on performance and ultimately profit, and it is all the more powerful because its significance is largely unrecognised.

To begin to fully understand its impact on effective leadership and engagement, we must first understand exactly what ego is and so its influence over our everyday behaviours, perceptions and responses.

What is Ego?

The most common understanding of ego is as a person's sense of self-esteem or self-importance. In this respect it often has negative connotations, used as a descriptor for an over inflated sense of pride or feelings of superiority in relation to others. It is certainly true for our purposes that ego often manifests itself in this way; but there are other ways of defining ego.

In *A New Earth*, Eckhart Tolle describes ego as 'a conglomeration of recurring thought forms and conditioned, mental-emotional patterns that are invested with a sense of 'I', a sense of self', and it is this definition of ego that is most appropriate to our explorations of leadership and it is the one to which I refer throughout this book.

For the purposes of our development as transformational leaders able to motivate and engage employees and deliver exceptional results, we must see ego as our sense of self-concept. This self-concept is the sum of all our experiences, the beliefs we have inherited and formed and the values we have developed.

It is an identity that starts developing in our very earliest years, and this very powerful sense of self is in fact a reflection of how others see us. If others see us as loveable and reflect this back to us, over time we develop an ego which sees itself as loveable; and if the world seems to abuse us, our ego can begin to see itself as worthless. Ego develops subconsciously as part of our normal psychological development and it is a reflection of how we think others see us, the sum of our experiences and beliefs about other people's reactions to and perceptions of us.

That is the real point. Ego is only ever a reflection, like the image we see in a pool of water, and comprises only of layers and layers of conditioning. As such it is actually a purely artificial construct and illusory concept, and our true self, or essence, lies beyond the ego.

The mask we wear

Our ego, or sense of self, develops as a response to the attitudes and events we encounter. From childhood, as we begin to challenge boundaries and explore the world around us, we become intensely aware of other people's reactions to our actions and ideas. Very often these responses appear negative; a parent's constant use of the word 'no' as they try to protect us from harm, or a schoolmaster's warning about our errant behaviour.

Our natural response to these perceived judgements is to begin to bury the 'offending' behaviour. We may, for example, stifle our creativity, limit our ambition or try to hide our vulnerability. In its place we create a 'mask', a way of behaving that wins us appreciation, approval or acceptance. This mask is a coping strategy; we pretend to be one thing so people cannot see who we fear we really are, and the longer we adopt the mask, the more we believe that *is* who we really are and the more worried we become that people might look behind and see our 'true', and unacceptable, self.

Case History - The Mask at Work:

Bruce was a Vice President of a large multinational company. He was well liked and respected within his organisation, but tended to avoid dealing with very difficult and awkward issues. During the course of our work together, we uncovered a typical mask. Bruce believed himself to be 'powerless' and compensated for this by 'pretending' to be collaborative; this was in fact a means of gaining approval and a typical ego-based behaviour. Transformation of this limiting belief led Bruce towards becoming a more relaxed and authentic leader, free from the need to seek approval and attention for himself and able to be more assertive as the task required.

In a leadership context, although the mask gives us safety, it can also be very limiting, and we can all recognise its manifestations. For example, someone who fears they are weak pretends to be powerful. They soon find this powerful persona is successful in keeping them happy and safe and seems to attract approval and acceptance; because it is successful they develop it further and further and hide behind the mask more and more. A perfect example of the negative manifestations of this powerful persona, if taken to an extreme and developed until it has gone too far, is the emergence of a bully. A successful strategy for an individual now leaves a trail of destruction in its wake and has negative impact on others through bullying relationships, whether those be in the home or workplace.

Similarly, someone who fears failure becomes less and less inclined to be creative, take risks or make decisions in case they make the wrong choice and attract criticism; from the ego's point of view it is far better to be a safe pair of hands than make mistakes. As a consequence, they risk becoming over-controlling, conservative or risk averse.

By the time we have been practicing these behaviours for 20 to 30 years, the patterns are deeply ingrained. We have forgotten our true self and instead see reality as who we fear we are; not good enough, smart enough, outgoing enough, handsome enough, worthy enough, successful enough, or creative enough. In short, we experience only a deeply conditioned sense of self or ego underpinned by low levels of self acceptance, self worth and self trust.

We also have deeply embedded and subconscious strategies we use to prove to ourselves we are acceptable, lovable and worthy; not who we fear we are. It is very hard to let go of these subconscious strategies. Very often the coping strategies of senior leaders have been incredibly successful in getting them where they are today, winning them power, money, success and acclaim. One of the difficulties with working to let go of those strategies is the fear that the success might melt away too.

It will not. Letting go of these strategies and our conditioned sense of self will open up a whole new level of leadership and deliver better performance and results than could ever be possible when we hold them close. The simple fact is ego often runs the show without our conscious awareness, and it is a powerful but often largely negative influence.

The destructive power of ego

We all have an ego and ego can be both constructive and helpful. However, all too often ego is actually destructive and restricts our ability to perform to the best of our own abilities and to lead others effectively. It is this destructive side of ego and its impact on our performance as leaders that we are addressing here. Ego-full leadership unbalances relationships, erodes trust, feeds fear and impedes performance and is responsible for many of the most pressing and difficult problems we face either in business or as societies.

Ego-full leadership is geared towards self survival and relies largely on negative behaviours such as control, manipulation, dominance, exploitation, risk aversion, avoidance and blame. It results in such issues as a lack of trust, ongoing power struggles and a fear of tackling difficult issues and ultimately hinders performance both at an individual and organisational level.

Teams and organisations subject to ego-full leadership are driven by fear and are lacking in creativity and innovation, often risk averse and in danger of falling behind their competitors.

Case History - The Destructive Ego

Jonathan is a senior executive in a healthcare organisation. He had the insight to understand that he was seen as 'cold' and 'hard' by his colleagues and in particular, his direct reports. He had become well-known for his angry outbursts. When we spoke, he appeared detached from his team referring to them as 'that lot'. This anger and detachment was born of frustration with, and resentment of, their poor performance.

Yet, when we looked more deeply, we uncovered the fact that when Jonathan had first joined the organisation he had, through his own fear of failure, become dominating and over controlling, micromanaging his staff. This generated dependency in his team which he then came to resent. Becoming aware of this and addressing his own fear of failure allowed Jonathan to begin to rebuild independence and confidence in his direct reports.

Ego and the bottom line

I have witnessed that the presence of ego is inversely proportional to leadership effectiveness in terms of engagement, innovation and individual performance; but emerging research clearly shows ego also has a profound impact on the bottom line.

In their pioneering book Egonomics, David Marcum and Steven Smith reveal some startling facts. More than half (51 per cent) of business leaders currently estimate ego costs companies between 6 and 15 per cent of annual revenue and a fifth (21 per cent) say the cost actually ranges between

16 and 20 per cent; and the majority (63 per cent) say ego has a negative impact on performance on an hourly or daily basis while a further 31 per cent see a weekly impact.

So it is clear that tackling the negative impacts of ego makes sound business and economic sense as well as bringing wider benefits in terms of stronger relationships and greater personal fulfilment.

> *More than half of business leaders say ego costs companies between 6 and 15 per cent of annual revenue and the majority say it has a negative impact on performance on an hourly or daily basis.*
> Egonomics, David Marcum and Steven Smith

The Ego in action

We know ego has a negative impact on individuals, teams and organisations, but what does it look like? Ego has many faces, all of which are familiar to us. Some are immediately obvious; for example, the bully is probably the most painful manifestation of ego in the office for most of us as their behaviour is so domineering and destructive. Other manifestations are less obvious but equally powerful; the procrastinator, the victim and the perfectionist may not be as immediately recognisable as ego-centred but that is exactly what they are.

Different masks have very different behaviours and traits associated with them, but there is one common and significant thread: fear.

The Bully

The Bully or tyrant is probably the most readily recognisable manifestation of ego and we have all come across someone like this whether at work, school or in other areas of our day to day lives.

A dominant character, the Bully tends towards aggressive and threatening behaviour and confuses power and authority. Literally or metaphorically puffing his or her chest out, the Bully is more than capable of using intimidating body language and words. It is not unusual to hear the Bully shouting or issuing threats, or to see them pointing a finger, as he or she homes in on and exploits colleagues' and associates' insecurities and perceived weaknesses.

"Attack is the best form of defence" is the motto which best defines this character who mistakenly believes they look stronger as a result of undermining and exposing others. Colleagues spend much of their time on tenterhooks, constantly anticipating the next accusation or outburst.

Divisive, accusatory and incapable of building authentic or productive working relationships, bullies leave a trail of destruction behind them and a legacy of mistrust, fear and underperformance.

Whilst the Bully puts great effort into building him or herself up and outward displays of what they perceive to be strength, beneath it all, just as with the other characters, the Bully's behaviour is rooted in fear and he or she feels deeply insecure.

The Victim

At the opposite end of the scale to the Bully, the Victim is almost totally passive, seeing life as something that happens to them and over which they have little or no control.

The world is a hostile place to the Victim and others are responsible for everything that happens to them, particularly negative events and influences. Self-responsibility, on the other hand, is an entirely alien concept. Self-deprecating and seemingly unconcerned by personal glory, the Victim is actually quick to blame others, and courage is in short supply.

The Victim is happiest following others because this shields them from personal exposure, decision making and the need to take responsibility for themselves or their actions. Familiar phrases falling from the Victim's lips include: "It's not my fault," "I didn't know," and "It's just the way it is."

Creativity, innovation and risk-taking and are all stifled by the Victim's fear of making decisions and taking responsibility. Change is threatening to them because it might reveal their fallibility and expose their shortcomings.

Fear pulls the Victim's strings. Self-responsibility risks uncomfortable self-exposure and self-knowledge.

The Control Freak

The Control Freak finds it hard to trust colleagues or to let them get on with their jobs. Their tendency towards micro-management is intensely frustrating for employees whose own creativity and development is stifled and who feel underrated and undervalued.

Looking over people's shoulders, constant checking and taking over tasks originally trusted to others are all typical behaviours of the Control Freak who has an obsessive need to be in charge of people, things and situations.

Creativity, engagement and job satisfaction all fall victim to the Control Freak's need to manage the minutiae of every project.

A brittle character that operates under tremendous stress, the Control Freak is fearful of one small mistake bringing the whole house of cards crashing down around them.

Ego manifests itself as intense fear in the Control Freak, who is motivated almost exclusively by a terror of failure or exposure.

The Procrastinator

The Procrastinator's main characteristics are conservatism and indecision. We have all seen them in action, sitting on the fence in meetings, happy to make the case for various courses of action but reluctant to put their head above the parapet when it comes to taking decisions.

Although the Procrastinator can be very black and white in his or her thinking, seeing things as 'right' or 'wrong' rather than in shades of grey, they find it hard to be equally robust in other areas. Decision-making is particularly difficult for them, and he or she can spend days weighing up options and then finding reasons not to act.

They retreat into dithering when facing challenging situations, loathe to take risks, to commit to a particular strategy or to have their name associated with a decision. Why do today what could be done tomorrow, is the fallback position of the Procrastinator who would rather live with the agony of endless deliberation than actually put their neck on the line. If they are forced to take a decision, they will do everything they can to find someone else to endorse their approach and share the responsibility.

Risk-taking, creativity and progress are all stifled by the Procrastinator's default position of inaction. Ironically, it is the Procrastinator's strong need to make the right decision, and their fear of failure, that stops them taking any decisions at all.

The Perfectionist

The Perfectionist is his or her own harshest critic. They drive themselves hard and expect nothing short of the very best results. A hard taskmaster, they demand the same high standards from colleagues as they do from themselves.

The perceptions and judgments of others are of paramount importance to the Perfectionist, and they invest a huge amount of emotional energy in worrying about how people see them. Driven by a fear of not making the grade, failure is simply not an option for them.

This constant pursuit of perfection often leads to unproductive management styles, and the Perfectionist displays the same suffocating iron grip on tasks and teams as the Control Freak. Driving people and teams to the limit, they dictate the pace and micro-manage every step of the process.

They are often heard seeking praise or approval, and can focus on the smallest detail or flaw whilst ignoring the greater success. The Perfectionist is driven almost exclusively by the fear of failure, exposure or not being deemed good enough.

The masks outlined here may seem extreme to some of us, but the fact is we will all recognise them, or at least elements of them, in those we work with and in ourselves. If they do seem extreme when read dispassionately, it is simply because we become so deeply ingrained in our ego or self concept, we will go to extreme lengths to defend it. However, the protective strategies we use often evolve subconsciously and we are unaware we are driven by them. They can also appear to be a very successful way of operating.

One of the difficulties in convincing leaders to embrace a more ego-less style is exactly that; they have achieved a good deal of success with their habitual modus operandi. Yet my experience of coaching leaders suggests that if you think you are successful now, I guarantee your full potential is being held hostage by your ego. I do not want you to take my word for it, but maybe these words will prick your curiosity enough for you to begin to think about and explore it for yourself. This is the way of the *Conscious Leader*.

One of the difficulties in convincing leaders to embrace a more egoless style is that they achieved a good deal of success with their current modus operandi. Yet the research evidence and my experience suggests that if you think you are successful now, I guarantee your full potential is being held hostage by your ego. I do not want you to take my word for it, but maybe these words will prick your curiosity enough for you to begin to think about and explore it for yourself. This is the way of the Conscious Leader.

A new model of leadership

We have examined the negative impact of ego-full leadership and its detrimental effect on profits and individual and team performance is clear. Ego-full leadership risks creating division, undermining morale and putting working relationships under unnecessary stress.

So, what are the benefits of taking ego out of the leadership equation and how do we begin to achieve this?

Moving beyond ego

> *Everything can be taken from a man but one thing; the last of the human freedoms - to choose one's attitude in any given set of circumstances, to choose one's own way.*
> Viktor E Frankll

We have seen that fear is the emotional trademark of the ego. Fear of failure, fear of judgment and fear of exposure are all manifestations of the ego at work. Most of us are well acquainted with at least one of these emotions. Those we do not recognise in ourselves we can often recognise in the attitudes and behaviours of others.

In short, fear and ego are inextricably linked. If we diminish ego, we diminish fear, because the ego's need to protect itself from external threats engenders fear as the predominant emotion. Also linked to ego are the many other fear-based behaviours and emotions with which we are all familiar, from anger to impotence and from exercising excessive control to absolving ourselves of responsibility altogether.

We have seen examples of the ego in action, in 'masks' and behaviours ranging from the bully to the victim. If our consciousness is based in ego, fear becomes both our constant companion and our master. This fear pervades our whole being, and directs our approach to life and so our approach to leadership. It undermines our very sense of self, rocking our self trust and thus feeding ego and strengthening further the masks we adopt.

Nowhere is this ego-based fear more powerful than in our working lives. All too often, it is this fear that has driven us to where we are now, that in our minds has helped us achieve success, status, wealth, advantage or whatever else we feel defines us. Letting go of fear or ego and the attitudes and behaviours it drives seems to the ego-full mind to risk letting go of all we have achieved; if we remove the mask, surely we risk seeing all we have achieved melt away.

The simple fact is it will not. Far from threatening all we have achieved, embracing ego-less, fearless leadership will bring new and manifold benefits. Limiting beliefs are always ego-based. Freeing ourselves of ego brings freedom, trust and authenticity, benefiting not just ourselves but those we lead and those we serve. It is enlightened, liberating and provides the bedrock for personal and group development and transformation. In embracing ego-less leadership we choose to build our foundations in rock, rather than in sand.

Case History - Loosening Ego's Hold

Dominic was the CEO of an international, mid-sized pharmaceutical company. Although well liked by his colleagues, he was described as overly precise, directive, constrained, inflexible and controlling. He had a tendency to step in, take over and focus excessively on detail and it was clear that this was eroding trust in key relationships at work. Having become aware of this, Dominic wanted to 'redefine his brand' and become a more relaxed and genuine leader.

As we worked together, we 'surfaced' Dominic's tendency towards perfectionism – another ego-based behaviour. This fed his tendency to adopt a pacesetting style, overlooking the needs of others. Ultimately, loosening the grip of this conditioned pattern resulted in a leader who was much more focused on the needs of his followers and who consequently generated much higher levels of trust and engagement in his direct reports.

Confronting fear

To begin to move towards an ego-less way of being and leading we must confront some of our deepest and most closely held, and often unrecognised, beliefs. This is not easy, and as we seek to tackle these beliefs it is almost certain our ego will rear its head in resistance.

This is not surprising. Our fear based behaviours and beliefs, whether they manifest themselves as aggression or reticence, are designed by ego to keep us safe. But in setting ego aside and so removing its control of our actions and reactions, our defensive behaviour subsides. The results are intensely liberating. Our need to control and manipulate other people and situations diminishes; and this frequently goes hand in hand with a new preparedness to step into unknown or ambiguous situations. As we realise we need not be defined by our fear we find a new willingness to step out of our comfort zones and to take greater risks.

Case History - Letting our fears define us

Robert is an executive director of a UK-based company. Early on in his career he had experienced a particularly traumatic event which had seriously undermined his trust in his ability to judge others accurately. Almost overcompensating, he had developed a tendency to be highly judgemental when first meeting people, immediately placing them in boxes labelled 'okay' or 'not okay', and with little prospect of ever being reassigned no matter what the evidence. It was also clear that those labelled 'not okay' were deemed as unworthy in some way, limiting the amount of time and energy that Robert was prepared to invest in these relationships. This ego-based behavioural trait became highly career limiting because Robert was unable to develop the wide range of strong stakeholder relationships demanded at the very highest level of business.

Ending separation

The more developed our ego, the stronger our sense of self. The more defined the boundaries between the self and others, the more separate we feel from them. We have all experienced, at some point or another, a sense of apartness. In some of us, ego has nurtured emotional isolation as a means of keeping ourselves safe. If we put emotional barriers between us and the world, we are less easily buffeted by the whims and actions of others and less exposed to the vagaries of circumstance.

> *Our deepest fear is not that we are inadequate. Our deepest fear is that we are powerful beyond measure. It is our light, not our darkness that frightens us most.*
> Marianne Williamson

As ego subsides and we re-establish a sense of oneness, we also re-establish a sense of interconnectedness with the world around us. As we begin to recognise this oneness, we begin to move into a whole new way or level of being. This is probably best expressed as becoming connected with our basic, unconditioned nature again and takes us into a whole new level of consciousness. The consciousness associated with this unconditional self is rooted in such qualities as compassion, peace, security and purpose, and the corresponding choices and behaviours that we are likely to make are wholly different, more nourishing and sustaining.

To use an analogy, when we operate from our ego we see ourselves as individual drops of water, separate from the ocean. When we move beyond our ego and connect to our soul, we appreciate the individuality of each molecule of water, of each wave on the surface, but we also know we are still part of that same ocean; still made of the same atoms and inextricably part of the whole.

> *When we operate from our ego we see ourselves as individual drops of water, separate from the ocean. When we move beyond our ego and connect to our soul, we appreciate the individuality of each molecule of water, of each wave on the surface, yet we know that we are still part of the same ocean; still made of the same atoms and inextricably part of the whole.*

Characteristics and behaviours of
Conscious Leaders

Conscious Leadership is a practical model for ego-less leadership, setting out clear steps for moving beyond the ego and becoming a truly transformational leader. The benefits of this model of leadership are manifold, both for individuals and for teams and organisations.

Organisations see improved performance and productivity. Employees are more engaged and better understand common goals, and they are more committed to achieving them. Increased creativity and improved problem solving on the part of individuals and teams benefit the whole organisation. In short, companies with senior leaders who lead from a *Conscious Leadership* perspective attract talent, foster talent and retain more talent and so create a real competitive edge.

Conscious Leaders themselves are calm, measured and have a deep understanding of themselves and others. In choosing to heal and transcend ego, a leader is no longer bound to the masks, behaviours and patterns and language of his or her ego. As ego fades, a more robust sense of self develops leading to a more balanced approach to life and work, to a higher level of performance and new and stronger leadership qualities. As fear dissolves, so the language and behaviours of the *Conscious Leader* begin to emerge. 'We' becomes more important than 'me', and the leader spontaneously finds they are genuinely impelled to serve.

Before moving on, perhaps it will be useful to define leadership as I see it in the *Conscious Leadership* model. True leadership is about removing the obstacles and resistances that get in the way of your followers achieving a common goal. In such ego-less leadership, we are more likely to see leaders who work for the greater good and motivate, reward and celebrate the success of others. Leaders develop greater personal resilience and bring clarity to confusion and calm to chaos. They create a sense of shared purpose which more deeply engages followers, and they build strong, empathetic relationships rooted in loyalty and trust.

> *True leadership is about removing the obstacles and resistances that get in the way of your followers achieving a common goal.*

Conscious, or ego-less, leaders speak authentically and seek to share the truth. They are collaborative, using the skills of others as well as their own talents for the purpose of collaborative problem solving, and they are fearless in their engagement with difficult issues. They help develop others to the very best of their potential, benefiting individuals' prospects and performance as well as improving the performance of the wider team.

They are more acutely sensitive to the needs of others and more aware of unspoken agendas, and they create working environments that support creativity, innovation and reward risk-taking. They bring balance and so create more sustainable working environments, and those they lead feel valued, supported and respected and have a clear sense of purpose.

The net result is real team work, where people's talents are used to the full and diversity is valued.

Organisational rewards

The potential positive impact of *Conscious Leadership* on individuals and teams is evident and almost impossible to dispute. It is not too hard to begin to extrapolate what the consequences might be for the well-being of the wider organisation.

An organisation that embraces ego-less leadership and manages to harness a critical tipping point in transforming its culture to one of *Conscious Leadership* is open to a whole host of benefits, not least increased performance and productivity across the board.

Conscious Leaders are better able to communicate vision and build trust. As employees become more engaged, their understanding of and commitment to organisational vision increases and individual and team effort improves. Employees with a clear sense of purpose and belonging and whose efforts and skills are recognised by their leaders are naturally more loyal to the organisation of which they are part and so retention rates improve and highly skilled, talented and committed individuals are more easily recruited even in intensely competitive markets.

Conscious Leadership creates trust and delivers more sustainable working environments. As employees begin to develop a belief in the organisation itself and its leadership, resilience and determination improves and a fundamental commitment to delivering the very best results develops. As trust increases, so more profitable and sustainable work environments are created.

Leaders who put 'we' before 'me' create teams of empowered, engaged employees whose creativity and skills are recognised. Employees who work in an environment where risk taking is encouraged will contribute more actively to problem solving. Operating in an entirely supportive environment free from fear, ridicule or blame, these same employees will be better equipped to prioritise effectively and make the best decisions to the benefit of the wider organisation.

Of course, the benefits extend beyond the organisation itself. *Conscious Leadership* naturally creates the levels of trust and transparency necessary to strong relationships with external as well as internal stakeholders, and the power of this cannot be under-estimated, both in terms of better serving customers and communities and in remaining engaged and profitable in intensely competitive times. When we lead from ego people around us are hesitant, anxious or pandering and reluctant to give honest feedback; ego-less leadership results in strong relationships, high levels of trust, genuine collaboration and better performance.

In short, *Conscious Leadership* allows for the rebuilding of organisational trust to the benefit of employees, customers, communities and to the organisation itself. Set out this clearly, it is hard to see an alternative.

The Choice

The choice we face is a simple one: do we lead from the ego or do we seek to gently set the ego aside, transcend it and so lead from an expanded, authentic self? Do we allow fear to drive us, or do we make a conscious decision to set fear aside and move forwards towards an ego-less way of leadership and embrace all the benefits it brings? Do we look towards a new model of leadership able to deliver increased organisational trust, better performance and greater profits and that benefits individuals as well the organisation; or, do we carry on as we are?

For me, there can only be one answer. To forfeit the opportunity of embracing ego-less leadership is to squander not only our own full potential but also the full potential of those we lead. To fully develop and embrace all that is possible we must look to a new ego-less way of leadership. If you too have chosen ego-less leadership as your preferred course, you are ready to begin the *Conscious Leadership* journey.

This book sets out a four step programme to deliver *Conscious Leadership* by gently setting the ego aside and becoming a truly transformational leader. It requires energy, motivation and commitment, and it is not a journey for the fainthearted; but the rewards it brings are far-reaching.

Key characteristics of Conscious Leaders

- Lead effectively, bravely and calmly; even in the most difficult and pressured circumstances
- Show a genuine respect for those they lead because they know that to truly lead people is to serve them as well
- Intuitively know that much of what is achieved comes through them rather than from them - they show humility
- Always put the good of the wider organisation before their own personal success

- Acknowledge their own vulnerabilities openly
- Operate with clear intent
- Are able to deal with underperformance fairly, respectfully and without procrastination

Personal benefits of Conscious Leadership

- Greater personal resilience
- Brings clarity where there was confusion and calm where there was chaos
- Creates purpose which more deeply engages followers
- Facilitates strong, empathetic relationships, creating loyalty and trust
- Develops your authentic voice and brings truth and realism to relationships and creativity and trust to collaborative problem solving
- Helps develop others to the very best of their potential
- More acute sensitivity to and awareness of unspoken agendas
- Creates balance and so creates more sustainable working environments

Organisational benefits of Conscious Leadership

- Increased performance and productivity
- Enhanced employee engagement
- Improved retention
- Better problem solving capabilities
- Improved decision-making and prioritisation
- Dealing with issues early
- Creating competitive edge

The tipping point

- Organisational trust rebuilt
- Employees committed to realising the organisational vision
- Belief in the organisation's leadership
- Profitable and sustainable environments

Part Two

The Conscious Leadership *journey*

The Conscious Leader*ship journey*

The *Conscious Leadership* model takes us through four key stages or levels of development associated with the evolution of a *Conscious Leader*. These stages are mutually dependent, and to move to the final state of *Conscious Leadership* in which ego is set aside and we emerge as truly transformational leaders, we must pass through the three intermediary stages.

Each of these states of consciousness has its own characteristic traits and or 'rites of passage' through which I believe we must journey before evolving into the next stage. It is simply not possible to skip a stage and still fulfil our potential to become *Conscious Leaders*. However, the rate of movement through each level and the propensity to cycle back round through the levels is unique to each individual.

It may well be the case that as we develop, expand and take on new challenges and so move out of our comfort zone, our ego comes to the fore again. If this does happen, and it is not unusual, it may be necessary to go back to an earlier level and re-establish our foundations.

In this sense, the *Conscious Leadership* model is not strictly linear, but more a cycle of development and growth. As we move through each stage, we are supported to engage more deeply with who we really are and so, in the process, move naturally from a predominantly ego-full towards an ever more ego-less style of leadership until ego can be consciously transcended.

Fundamentally, the *Conscious Leadership* model takes leaders through a process of transformation or healing, a making whole. The first two stages remain very much about the ego or self and then in the final two stages we begin to transcend the ego and in doing so open up a host of new possibilities both for ourselves and for those we lead and serve.

It is when the process of healing, or making whole, is complete and the ego has been set aside that we have finally and fully prepared the ground to become truly exceptional and transformational leaders.

Stage One
Transforming the Ego

When we set out on the first stage of our journey towards ego-less leadership, we find ourselves operating at the level of *Dysfunctional Ego*.

We have already examined the concept of ego; what it is and how it is formed. In terms of motivation, one of the core drivers of the ego is, as I have said, to keep us safe. Understanding this is vital to our successful interpretation of the behaviours we see in anyone operating at this level.

I have also already defined the types of behaviours we are likely to see at this stage, encompassing those of both the 'aggressive' and 'passive' ego types, and I have established that the common factor behind these behaviours is fear. In my experience, low levels of self trust, self worth and self acceptance create the fractured and defensive sense of self I refer to as the *dysfunctional ego*.

In building strong foundations of self trust, self worth and self acceptance we are able to transform fear and self doubt. In its place we build and nourish confidence in ourselves and in our choices. This must not be confused with arrogance, bravado or misplaced confidence. It is something altogether simpler and fundamental which is the foundation for the emergence of functional ego.

How is Your Ego showing up?

These questions begin to give you an insight into your own ego traits and how your ego shows up most strongly. It is essential you answer these questions according to what you really feel and how you experience yourself in reality, rather than how you want or hope to be or by choosing what you think might be the 'right' answer. The more honest you can be with yourself in this profile the more accurate the benchmark. These questions act as a marker to help you identify common types of ego-full behaviour.

- Do you feel worthy of success?
- Do you feel that you have to prove yourself, either to yourself or to others?
- Are you comfortable sharing and showing your weaknesses to others?
- Do you trust yourself to get out of a difficult situation?
- Are you able to relax knowing that everything will be okay?
- Do you feel comfortable with conflict?
- Do you agree or disagree with the statement "I'm comfortable with taking risks"?
- Do you agree or disagree with the statement "I'm comfortable with ambiguous situations"?
- Do you agree or disagree with the statement "I'm comfortable with being wrong"?
- Do you agree or disagree with the statement "I often fear not being good enough or being found out"?
- Do you agree or disagree with the statement "I get very uncomfortable in situations which seem to be out of my control"?

- Do you agree or disagree with the statement "My tendency is listening to others' ideas and allowing these to shape my thinking in pursuit of a better outcome"?

- Do you agree or disagree with the statement, "My default pattern is to treat people equally; I do not tend to exclude people or put people in boxes"?

- Are you happy to:
    - Admit when you are wrong about something?
    - Admit when you have made a mistake?
    - Say sorry?
    - Allow people to see your vulnerabilities and weaknesses?
    - Admit you do not have all the answers?
    - Be yourself even when that goes against the crowd?

- Do you often use the pronoun 'I' rather than 'we' when talking about work projects?

- Do you trust others to behave with integrity towards you?

- Are you making decisions based on your own needs of those of the wider organisation?

- Is your motivation your own personal glory or the greater good?

You will find it useful to revisit these questions throughout your *Conscious Leadership* journey. Honest answers will give you a realistic picture of where you are and the progress you have made.

Self preoccupation

Before we can begin to put this confidence in place we must first deal with the self preoccupation common to many leaders at the first stage of the *Conscious Leadership* journey.

When we operate from the territory of Dysfunctional Ego we are almost wholly preoccupied with ourselves and our own story. We spend a great deal of time thinking about our actions and often shape ourselves to fit what we imagine others think and/or expect from us. This, to the dysfunctional ego, secures our survival.

Actually, these behaviours stem from low levels of self confidence. Our self worth, self trust and self acceptance are in short supply and consequently we are bound by but terrified of the judgments of others. Why are we both dependent on and afraid of these judgments? Simply because, at the Dysfunctional Ego stage we fear our self image will be threatened or attacked and what we most fear about ourselves will be revealed.

Despite the emphasis we place on the judgments of others, we ourselves are the only true focus of our attention; it is our own insecurities, neuroses and foibles on which we concentrate. Other people are only part of the picture in so far as they feed these manifestations of ego. The welfare and needs of these colleagues and associates are of scant importance to us and we give them little thought.

Since leadership is fundamentally all about meeting the needs of others, those we lead and those we serve, we can see clearly how restricted a leader so preoccupied with themselves must be. When we are tied up in playing the starring role in a drama of our own making, we simply cannot prioritise and meet the needs of others or help them fulfil their potential. Ironically, nor can we ever hope to fulfil our own potential when operating at this restricted level.

The way beyond this paralysing, although often unwitting, self-obsession is through rebuilding our foundations. We need to establish a genuine and fundamental sense of confidence in ourselves, built not on the judgments, or perceived judgments, or reactions of others or on the material trappings of success. Rather we need to build a genuine sense of self worth, self trust and self acceptance.

Case History - The negative power of self-preoccupation

Rebecca was an incredibly shy person and entirely preoccupied with how others judged her, wrongly thinking everyone else was constantly observing, judging and ultimately probably condemning her performance. This was particularly noticeable with people she did not know and in meetings, because of her shyness and fears about other people's thoughts, she said very little.

As a result, she became incredibly self-conscious. This served to exacerbate her shyness and led her to withdraw even further. Here, a low level of self worth and self acceptance led to a complete preoccupation with self, something which is very typical in people at the dysfunctional ego stage of development.

The Three Pillars of Confidence

In order to be truly open to the world, move beyond our preoccupation with self and so lay the foundations for exceptional, ego-less leadership, a fundamental self confidence must be in place. Without it, we risk reverting quickly into the defensive behaviours of the ego and find our actions and reactions once again driven by fear.

Interestingly, confidence in one form or another is lacking in the vast majority of leaders. No matter what an individual's agenda or goals are, as we begin to peel away the layers and move towards the root of an issue we invariably find one or more of what I refer to as the Three Pillars of Confidence are missing or under developed. These are the pillars upon which a healthy ego can comfortably stand, and the presence or absence of each of these pillars defines whether our ego is in effect at a functional or dysfunctional level.

Without these three pillars we are almost constantly in fight or flight mode, our dysfunctional ego using these mechanisms as a form or self protection. Building these pillars creates the foundation of feeling safe and robust enough for the ego to let go of fear and lower its defences and so evolve towards the next development milestone.

These pillars are the key strands of a fundamental level of confidence. In order to begin the journey towards a more authentic way of being we must begin by working to build and strengthen each of these pillars.

Building self worth

At the root of low self worth often lies a limiting belief about not being good enough. Most of us have at some point in our careers been able to relate to this. It might be that we suffer from 'impostor syndrome', believing that we have got where we are by some kind of happy accident and are constantly worried that one day we will be found out as lacking the skills and talent to do our jobs effectively; or it may simply be that we always feel the need to work that little bit harder or that little bit later to make up for what we believe to be our inadequacies.

To me, this belief of not being good enough is the mother of all limiting beliefs. It has a pervasive quality, infiltrating all aspects of our working lives, undermining our successes, magnifying any small slips in judgment and taking the edge off all that is good. It also leads us to constantly measure our achievements, talents and qualities against those of others and to constantly strive to prove ourselves worthy.

A leader operating at this level is therefore almost entirely externally referenced, as often so much store is given to others' judgments and opinions as he or she seeks the validation of others to prove his or her self worth. The impact on the way that this type of leader acts is significant. Externally referenced leaders are constantly second guessing what others want or expect and shape their behaviour to fit those perceived expectations. The process can be exhausting. It is also fundamentally flawed; we will never gain enough approval or validation to satisfy our dysfunctional ego and allay our fears.

So the first step in our journey must be to build and develop our sense of self worth. Key to this is learning to own our strengths, something many of us find surprisingly hard to do.

Owning our strengths - Exercises for building self worth

People who lack self worth are often more than happy to embrace all that they believe is wrong about them - their weaknesses, perceived failings and vulnerabilities - but are almost entirely dismissive of any positive attributes, skills or talents. They may find it hard to accept compliments with good grace or to believe positive comments about their performance.

These exercises are designed to help you challenge these warped perceptions and build a more realistic and positive view of your strengths.

Exercise One - Accepting compliments and recognising our strengths

We are all paid compliments from time to time, although many of us chose to ignore, belittle or forget them. Next time someone pays you a compliment, look them straight in the eye, take a deep breath and simply thank them. It is important to let the compliment emotionally 'land' with you; the tendency for those with low self worth will be to dismiss the comment out of hand or, at best, to say "thank you" quickly whilst simultaneously and subconsciously dismissing the compliment.

Dismissing a compliment serves to reaffirm our sense or worthlessness, not least because we are actually dismissing ourselves, but it also actually shows a lack of kindness and generosity towards the person who has taken the time to pay us the compliment in the first place.

For the second part of this exercise, gather a list of your own strengths and positive qualities; things you admire about yourself and recognise to be true. It may be easier and more effective to collect two qualities a week over five or six weeks. To do this you will need to become more aware of your positive thoughts and your behaviours towards both yourself and others. You will also begin to genuinely recognise there are things you are good at and which you can cherish as positive qualities.

Review this list on a daily basis, breathing life into the words so that when you read a word you remember the scenario associated with it and recognise this as an active quality. You need to become so familiar with the list and qualities in it that if anyone asked, you would be able to tell them all your strengths without difficulty or hesitation and truly recognise them as your qualities.

This is usually an entirely foreign concept for people with low self worth and who spend much of their time putting themselves down and ignoring their positive qualities. If this is you, then you must persevere with it. This exercise will be incredibly effective in helping you start valuing who you are right now. You can then start to gradually build a stronger sense of self worth and develop a more rational assessment of your strengths.

Building self trust

> *"Freedom isn't worth having if it doesn't include the freedom to make mistakes."*
> Mahatma Ghandi

As we have seen, fear is the emotional trademark of the ego, and this is particularly evident at the dysfunctional level. Nowhere is this fear more apparent than in relation to self trust. Fear of failure, fear of being criticised or condemned, of other people's judgments or our own perceived inadequacies, plagues us when we operate at this leadership level.

One of the root causes of this fear lies in low levels of self trust. This is manifested particularly in the form of fear of failure and our ability to cope with adverse events. If we did trust ourselves fully then we would know that whatever happens to us, and whatever challenges lie ahead, we will be equipped to deal with them.

The problem is that at dysfunctional ego level we do not inherently know this to be true. We live in fear of the next mistake, the next judgment or next catastrophe, although, of course, if we looked at the situation more calmly and logically we would realise these things very rarely ever actually happen. If we do make a mistake or fall short of the mark, at dysfunctional ego level we take this incredibly personally. Our first response is not to think a strategy or approach failed in a particular set of circumstances but rather to think 'I am a failure'.

Case History - The absence of trust

Paul is a high potential individual working in a multinational technology company. When we first met, one of his key leadership issues was his need to be in total control in meetings he chaired. He was fearful of debate, ambiguity and "things going off course" in case he could not bring them back on track. He imagined chaos would result and that this would reflect badly on him and others would judge him to be a failure.

Of course, what this all consuming need for control actually does is stifle creativity, squander the benefits that come from true diversity and hinder performance. Building trust, and first and foremost trust in oneself, is at the heart of transforming this issue.

One more aspect of self trust is worth attention. We spend so much of our time weighing up if and to what extent we should trust others, but this is an almost meaningless exercise unless we trust ourselves. Indeed, how do we believe in our assessments of others if we have little or no faith in ourselves? Self trust is an immensely powerful force. Without it we simply cannot begin to fulfil our true potential. Instead, we will hesitate, play small, hold back and invent numerous seemingly perfect reasons to justify our position.

"Trust me, if you aren't making mistakes, you're not learning - or, at least you're not learning enough."
Vineet Nayar

This is why cultivating self trust is so important. Once we have it, it will carry us through even the most challenging situations and allow us to overcome obstacles effectively. We will stop finding reasons why we cannot do things, but instead move forwards, achieve our goals and fulfil our potential.

> *"If I find 10,000 ways something won't work, I haven't failed. I am not discouraged, because every wrong attempt discarded is another step forward".*
> Thomas Edison

Exercises for developing self trust

The first step in developing self trust is to begin to identify the root causes of our lack of trust in ourselves. These might, for example, be a fear of failure, a fear of making a fool of ourselves, a feeling of inadequacy, a fear of being rejected or a combination of these fears. Working with a skilled professional coach will help you accurately identify these root causes, which often lie deep within the psyche and can be hard to recognise in oneself.

Once we have begun to identify what it is that undermines our self trust, we bring awareness to the problem, and this recognition is very often the first step towards loosening its grip on us. As with self worth, cultivating a nurturing and caring inner voice is an important starting point.

> *Exercise one - Developing an affirming inner voice*
>
> *This time, we look to replace the root cause of the problem with an affirming, supportive phrase. So, for example, we would replace a phrase such as "I am not good enough" with an affirming, supportive phrase such as "My best is good enough".*

Alternatively, we can replace limiting beliefs with something more positive and liberating, and actually more truthful. So, for example, we might take a limiting belief such as 'if I make a mistake I am a failure' and replace it with 'if I do make a mistake, I then have the opportunity to learn and grow' or 'making mistakes is an important part of the creative process' or simply 'I can make a mistake and still be okay'.

Exercise two - Collecting virtual mentors

This exercise is adapted from the work of Robert Dilts

Virtual mentors can be a very useful way of strengthening the beliefs we have been working on with the inner voice exercise. So, when building self trust, we may want to think of someone we know who conveys that sense of self trust very strongly.

Once we have someone in mind, we imagine this person standing next to or behind or in front of us, which ever feels most comfortable, and then simply step into their shoes. Once in their shoes, we take on their physiology and allow ourselves to feel how they feel. In this instance we may be feeling what it is like to have a strong sense of self trust, or to feel good enough or stress-free. Now look through their eyes and think about what message or advice your mentor would have for you.

Finally, step back into your own shoes and receive that message. As you receive it, concentrate on the feelings you sense as you experience greater self trust or feel you are good enough.

The great thing about these virtual mentors is that we can take them anywhere and everywhere with us and draw on their strength in a whole host of situations that challenge our self trust.

Exercise three - Separating the problem from our sense of self

Many of us who fear failure simply confuse failing in a particular task with actually being a failure. If we stop to think about this for a moment, we can quickly see how flawed our thinking is. Countless hugely successful people did not succeed the first time and made plenty of so called mistakes before hitting their own personal jackpot. Richard Branson, Thomas Edison and James Dyson, to name only a few, have had plenty of failures on the way to their great successes. They have not, however, let these failures define them.

Take some time to consider the growth and development of people you admire and respect, and think about what their attitude to failure might be and how you can learn from that and adopt a similar attitude. Failure is a form of feedback; it is as simple as that. Learn from it, use it as a building block for development and growth, but do not fear it.

Exercise four - Creating a powerful question

Very often we fear a vague notion that something awful might unfold if X happens or does not happen. However, if we bring our full attention to it and face fully the worst possible outcome, we see that it is not in fact as big or significant as feared and we could actually cope if it ever did come about.

Therefore a surprisingly powerful question to ask oneself is: What is the very worst thing that could happen? After asking the question and recognising the answer, simply ask yourself: "How could I cope with that?"

Usually when we do this, we see the worst-case scenario is actually something we can cope with and that life would go on.

Building self acceptance

Despite the very obvious career success of people in leadership positions and the outward trappings of success they accumulate along the way, many leaders still find that at the very deepest level they are unable to accept all of who they are. It is not uncommon for one facet of the self to become a particular focus for loathing, whether that be their feelings of shyness or a perceived lack of academic prowess. This same facet, seen as bad or a representation of some kind of failing or failure, is then totally rejected. It becomes a 'shadow' self, constantly disowned and repressed.

People often try to hide this 'shadow' at all costs, very often subconsciously, and feel immensely uncomfortable in situations which they see as exposing this weakness or requiring the quality they perceive as lacking in themselves. Often, the tendency for external referencing arises again and there can be a kind of mild paranoia as a leader feels, normally quite wrongly, that others are acutely aware of, focused on, and likely to exploit, these areas of weakness.

Often this process is accompanied by self flagellation. This concentration on one's perceived inadequacies and the tendency to beat oneself up is not only a waste of energy but also adds a further layer of discomfort, or in the Buddhist way of thinking could be said to add suffering to pain.

To move beyond the stage of dysfunctional ego and the preoccupation with self and begin to make ourselves whole again, we must understand a fundamental truth. Making whole is not about striving for perfection, but rather about understanding that being human is to be imperfect. Once we understand this and begin to accept our imperfections, their grip on us begins to loosen.

Exercises for developing self acceptance

The following exercises will begin to assist the process of learning to accept all of who you are.

Exercise one - Making whole

This exercise involves identifying those parts of ourselves we have suppressed, disowned or cut off. This is not always as simple as it first sounds, as many of these facets of our personalities are buried deep in our subconscious, and often the only sign of them is our harsh judgment of these traits in others. We also often over-compensate for these buried parts of ourselves, so actually 'over use' the opposite behaviour. We may, for, example, compensate for a fear of being selfish by spending a disproportionate amount of time caring for other people.

A number of questions might prove helpful in identifying these hidden parts. Try asking:

- *What would I rather other people didn't know about me?*
- *What parts of myself do I try to hide so I look good?*
- *What issues do I judge most harshly in other people and what might this say about my own fears?*
- *What part of my own 'shadow' does this most likely relate to?*

Exercise Two - A simple way of building self acceptance

Every day, preferably in the morning before you leave the house, look at yourself in the mirror. Be sure that you look directly into your own eyes - some people find this very difficult - and say to yourself with real feeling and emotion: I completely accept myself for all that I am or I fully accept all that I am without reservation.

If these phrases do not work well for you, adapt them or use your own form of words. It is important to keep this sentence simple, in the first person and in present tense. It must also be framed in the positive.

Firm foundations

The Three Pillars of Confidence are the fundamental building blocks of *Conscious Leadership*. They require diligent and committed attention if we are to progress on the journey towards truly transformational leadership, and it is likely you will revisit these early insights and exercises a number of times during the course of your development.

Most leaders, no matter how advanced they appear, need to work on at least one of the pillars; and the majority of us work on them all. This takes commitment and courage, but they are, in my view, the only route for developing as a truly mature, well balanced and effective leader. For those of you who are unsure whether your ego interferes with your leadership potential, seeking high quality, anonymous 360 degree feedback will help you see things more clearly.

These exercises will get you started and will prove a valuable resource throughout your journey, but I also recommend that, if at all possible, you work with a professional coach. This will help you see your blind spots and help keep you on course, revealing key insights and producing real movement more quickly.

Stage Two
Functional Ego

As we move from dysfunctional to functional ego we arrive at the second stage of the *Conscious Leadership* journey. The healing process of the first stage has focused on rebuilding and developing the Three Pillars of Confidence. As self worth, self trust and self acceptance develop, so the ego becomes increasingly whole. In turn, the shroud of fear that is ever present and pervasive during the dysfunctional ego phase begins to fall away and the functional ego emerges.

In my experience, it is an increasing sense of self acceptance which is the defining factor for a leader entering into this second stage of leadership. The process of coming to know and accept the 'shadow' side of ourselves comes strongly into play, and the result of this self acceptance is that the walls of defensiveness we have consciously or subconsciously built begin to fall away.

We become increasingly accepting of and realistic about both our strengths and our flaws; we no longer fear others noticing traits we once saw as weaknesses, traits that we felt we needed to hide at all costs. We are reaching the 'I'm OK; you're OK' state of being and this is intensely liberating to the leader, freeing up energy and creativity and a genuine ability to see beyond oneself.

One other much reported sign of progress is that, as people move forward and begin to develop the Three Pillars of Confidence and a more functional ego, they begin to become aware of others struggling with the same issues, patterns and behaviours they have struggled with in the past. When you find yourself in this position, you can be sure you are making progress.

Functional ego behaviours

> *All that we are is a result of what we have thought.*
> *Buddha*

The letting go of fear is of great significance not least because as fear subsides so does defensive behaviour. A leader moving into the functional ego leadership level becomes noticeably less controlling and does not feel the same need to manipulate situations or colleagues.

This frequently goes hand in hand with a new willingness to step into unknown or ambiguous situations. There is a greater willingness to step out of one's comfort zone and take greater risks. This type of behaviour would be almost inconceivable to a leader in the dysfunctional ego stage.

Perhaps even more striking are the internal changes that take place. Energy that has for so long been used to build and reinforce defensive walls is released and can be put to a more positive use. This is usually experienced as a tremendous relief and leaders at the functional stage often report feeling much happier, less stressed and more relaxed. Certainly, as the ego is increasingly healed, life becomes an easier and more pleasant experience.

However, at this second stage of leadership development, we are still firmly concerned with ego. Indeed, we need to continue to concentrate on the healing of the ego in order to prepare for the next stage of leadership. For this reason, leaders at this functional stage as well as those at the first, dysfunctional stage will still refer to 'I' and 'me', their language reflecting their continued involvement with the self. Similarly, at this stage we still see others predominantly in terms of their relationship to us; to our lives, our success and our security and how they can contribute to our own glory.

If we remain committed to growth, healing and becoming whole, we will move naturally towards the next level of leadership, that of the authentic leader. Readiness for the move to this next stage is characterised by the behaviours we have identified here and most notably the fact that a leader feels more relaxed, open and flexible. As a result, a leader will spontaneously begin to develop the capacity to think more about the needs of others rather than being focused wholly on meeting their own needs.

Exercises for developing functional ego

These exercises build on our work on the Three Pillars of Confidence, helping us to establish a more profound sense of our self worth, self trust and self acceptance. Continue with the earlier exercises whenever you need to, and work on the whole set of exercises until you have established the new thought patterns and behaviours associated with functional leadership.

Exercise One - Working with our inner voice

Most of us are familiar with the inner dialogue we have with ourselves, or our inner voice. For people with a low level of self worth this voice is often particularly harsh, critical and judgmental. Yet how we communicate with ourselves paves the way for supporting all of our subsequent efforts to build a healthy, functional ego.

How on earth can we build a healthy ego if we spend most of our time telling ourselves how stupid, ineffective or bad we are? For many of us, this inner voice has become our own worst enemy. Put simply, it is actually a form of self-abuse. Our aim now must be to turn this inner voice into our best and most supportive friend.

The good news is it is entirely possible to become master of one's own mind and in doing so change our inner dialogue and so our views of and experience of ourselves. In changing our internal experience of ourselves, we also change our perceptions of the world around us.

Step One: Become completely aware of your inner voice

Spend a fortnight simply listening to your inner voice. Note when and how it appears. Understand whether it is a voice that is familiar to you, whether your own or someone else's, and think about the significance of this. What does the voice say? Is it critical or judgmental and what tone or volume does it adopt?

This may seem rather simple or laboured, but it is incredibly important. Awareness is always the first step towards change and the more we recognise and understand our inner voice and bring it into the light, the more likely we are to dissolve its hold over us.

Step Two: Objectify this voice

The next stage is to objectify this voice. Hold your hand out in front of you and ask your inner voice to come out onto your hand. This may sound entirely ridiculous but it is amazing what appears for people. It may be an abstract object that can be seen, or even a miniature person; or it may be just a shape or colour, or even a feeling of heaviness or warmth. There is no right or wrong; it is simply whatever appears for you. Now give that object a label. This should be a single word which helps us objectify the voice. It could be a name like 'Mr Grumpy', for example, or it could be an abstract label such as 'resistance'.

Thank the voice for turning up. Express a willingness to develop a dialogue with it and to understand its intent. It is important to understand that no matter how critical or judgmental the voice may be, it is a part of you which is in some way (as far as it is concerned) looking out for you. Very often, its intention is to keep you safe.

Now open up a dialogue with your inner voice and listen carefully to what it has to say. It is always important that we listen with an open mind, for this in itself reduces the tension and conflict which has usually existed between the two parts of us, our self and our inner voice. You may also want to explain to the voice what your intent is for whatever behaviour you are trying to cultivate. Invite your inner voice to collaborate constructively with you to resolve the issue.

This is quite a complex task but the aim is to turn something from being largely subconscious and combative or destructive into something which is entirely conscious and collaborative. As a result, we begin to end the inner turmoil or war that has very often existed for many, many years.

Exercise Two - Adopt a voice

Another way of working with our inner voice that can be both incredibly powerful and fun is to replace the usual voice with something that is known as a 'comedy voice'. Here we select a familiar voice, perhaps a cartoon character or a real-life person we find extremely funny. We then substitute the usual voice with the comedy voice. So, now the inner voice is saying the same things but sounding completely ridiculous.

Very often we take our inner voice incredibly seriously, as if it is law, but when we introduce humour the hold it seems to have over us dissolves.

Of course, this exercise requires consistent practice and application over several weeks, if not months, before we start to fully transform the existing pattern. This is because we are working at conscious mind level. However, the good news is, you should start noticing benefits beginning to accrue quite quickly as each intervention will positively effect your state and ability to respond more effectively.

Exercise Three - Breathing in fear

One incredibly effective and well used way of tackling fear, or any other negative emotion, is to acknowledge and connect with it rather than fighting or hiding from it. Here we learn to tackle our fear by connecting with it through using an ancient Buddhist practice called Tonglen.

This exercise works through identifying our fearfulness or perhaps anger, connecting with it and then dissolving our fixation on it and consequently the chains of ego.

Firstly, identify the issue you want to deal with - whether its a specific frustration or a more general sense of anger, fear, inadequacy or heaviness - and then simply rest your mind for a moment or two. Start the exercise by focusing on texture. As you breathe in, feel a hot, dark heaviness; and, as you breathe out, exhale a cool, bright and light sense of freshness. Breathe in through every pore of your body, and radiate outwards through every pore. Continue with this until you feel totally synchronised with your breathing.

Now, begin to work on your personal issue or emotion. If this is fear, for example, breathe that in and then breathe out confidence and security, or any other emotion or state you would like to replace it with. Start doing this just for yourself and then after a couple of minutes expand it to include others. You can include anyone and everyone else experiencing the same issue. As you continue, make the taking in and sending out more and more profound.

Do not worry if, at this stage, you find connecting with others a challenge. We will do more of this later in the Six Practices of the Conscious Leader. For now, concentrate on transforming your own negative energy.

Exercise Four - Developing a resource state

This exercise is adapted from the work of Robert Dilts

Choose a resourceful state such as self-confidence or fearlessness you would like to experience more often, and then identify a specific time in your life in which you fully experienced that state. It does not matter when that time is; it could be at work, in leisure time, at school or even in childhood.

Now re-live that experience, associating yourself fully in your own point of view. See through your own eyes, hear through your own ears, and feel the sensations in your body. Take an inventory of the thoughts you had and your behaviours at the time, both obvious and subtle. Listen to any sounds or words associated with that memory. Look through your mind's eye at scenes and details of objects and events which make up that experience. Get in touch with the sensations, both emotional and tactile, associated with feeling resourceful. Notice your body posture, breathing and other aspects of your body and recall any smells or tastes related to the experience. When you have finished your inventory, stop thinking of the experience and shake off the state.

Next we need to select a unique self anchor. Identify some part of your upper body that is easy for you to touch, but which is not usually touched during daily interactions. An ear lobe, the knuckle of your ring finger, or the skin in between your forefinger and middle finger can be good areas for this as they are not often touched in normal day to day contact.

Start to re-access or relive the memory. When you feel the state is about to reach maximum intensity, touch or squeeze the part of your body that you have chosen as your anchor. Adjust the pressure of your touch or tightness of your squeeze to match the degree of intensity of your feeling of the resource state. After you have done this for a few seconds, stop thinking of the experience and shake off the state.

Now test your anchor by clearing your mind and simply touching or squeezing its location. The associated experience of your resource state should arise spontaneously without any conscious effort. If it does not, you need to repeat the proceeding stages of this exercise until it does. The strength of this anchor builds over time and the more you attach resourceful feelings to it, the more strongly you will be able to recall the state by touching the anchor.
You can now use this anchor to help you access a more resourceful state in other situations, as and when you need it.

Exercise Five - Objectifying the issue

This exercise involves objectifying the perception, experience or issue that is threatening a healthy sense of self trust.

Firstly, visualise the problem or the so-called failure that concerns you. Now take that visualisation and put it outside of yourself so you can see it on the table or the floor. Notice its size, colour, shape and movement. Are there any sounds associated with it? You may see the problem simply as a shape or symbol or maybe as an object.

Now imagine you are floating above the problem, perhaps seeing it as if you were a surveillance camera situated in a corner of a room. Notice the distance between you and the problem. Then take any feelings you have about it outside of your body, placing them firmly with the problem or failure.

When this is done, ask yourself the following question: If this issue/failure had a positive intention for me and there was something I might learn from it, what would that positive intention or message be? *Or you may want to ask:* If this problem was a friend, what message of support or learning might it have for me?

Exercise Six - Finding your shadow

This exercise is adapted from the work of Nick Williams

This is another exercise that can help you identify your shadow, or those elements of yourself you have repressed.

Imagine a newspaper reporter is writing a very critical and damning article about you. What would be the worst thing or things they could possibly say? What would really cut deeply?

You may even need or want to write the article yourself, but in the third person, to really get to grips with your deepest fears. These fears point directly towards the part of yourself you have disowned or buried in the name of gaining acceptance and approval.

Exercise Seven - Accepting lost fragments

This exercise is adapted from the work of Nick Williams

This exercise is all about reclaiming parts of ourselves we have cut off, bringing them into the light and creating a constructive dialogue with each and every part of ourselves.

Sit quietly somewhere you will not be disturbed. Make sure both your feet are resting on the floor that your hands are resting in your lap and your spine is well supported. Take a few moments to breathe deeply and just follow your breath in and out.

Then, in your mind's eye, imagine you are standing in a darkened room. This room has a single bright light at one end and you are standing under this light, fully illuminated. This means that you can see shadow areas in the distant corners of the room. Know that you are completely safe under this light.

When you are ready, invite that part of you about which you feel ashamed or guilty, all that you feel you try to hide from the world, out from the shadows and into the light. Invite it to come slowly towards you in its own time. Watch this part of yourself emerge from the shadows and take notice of the form it takes (this may be a thing, an object, a creature or a person) and watch how this part of you moves and how its energy looks and feels.

Continue to gently invite that part of yourself to come towards you and into the light. When it has, thank if for turning up. In your own mind give it a name or a label. Then apologise to it for having cut it off in the past and having kept it in the shadow. Ask its forgiveness. Listen to what it has to say.

Then ask your shadow part to explain what it is afraid of and try to understand how this part of you has been trying to keep you safe in some way. Understand that although the behaviour may be difficult and disruptive, the intention has always been positive. When your shadow part has finished speaking, briefly summarise to it in your own mind what you have heard it say. Then explain to your shadow part that you also want the same thing - in some way, shape or form to be safe - but you want to do it in a more fulfilling and effective way and with your shadow's support.

Ask that part of you for any ideas or thoughts about how you might best work together, creating a new way of being that fulfils both your intentions and yet creates more resource behaviours or internal emotional states. When you have finished your conversation reach out and physically connect with your shadow part. You may give it a hug, hold its hand or it may even dissolve into you to become part of you. Spend a few moments just enjoying the feeling of being reunited with a lost part of yourself.

Recognising the functional ego:

The behaviours we see when an individual reaches the level of functional ego are defined by the individual's greater level of self acceptance. These behaviours do not fulfil the largely defensive role of dysfunctional ego and so we see a leader who is more relaxed and flexible in approach and who is:

- Often more relaxed in situations that were once seen as threatening, including when managing critical meetings or difficult people
- Much happier with ambiguity or diversity
- Free from the need to be always be in control
- A better listener because they are less preoccupied with their own inner dialogue
- Aware their inner dialogue has shifted from being largely critical to largely supportive

- Feeling happier, more uplifted and energised; this is often related to the fact that these individuals are now less driven to prove themselves which is fundamentally draining
- Less concerned with what other people think about them and has instead started to use their own inner compass as their guide
- Happier to be bolder because they no longer associate a failure with being a failure; failure is instead now part of the learning process
- Aware of behaviours in others they had until recently struggled with themselves

Stage Three
The authentic leader

We have all met an authentic leader at some stage or another, although they remain relatively rare. It is partly their rarity value that makes them stand out from the crowd, but it is also because they possess the quality that many of us covet but which for most of us remains stubbornly elusive; they are truly comfortable in their own skin.

Authentic leaders are rooted in a state of quiet confidence, accompanied by an emerging humility; but the most notable characteristic of all at this stage is their willingness to be vulnerable. Where does this stem from? The fundamental shift that takes place as we move into authentic leadership level is that by now we have developed a very deep level of self acceptance.

This acceptance extends not only to a recognition of their strengths but also to areas of weakness; the authentic leader is equally accepting of both their light and their shadow sides. They have made friends with their so-called weaknesses and so their impact is diminished. Authentic leaders know they are just fine as they are.

Furthermore, authentic leaders have developed equanimity and true objectivity. They have an ability to separate themselves from a problem or issue. So, for example, when a project fails or does not work in the way expected or deliver the anticipated results, the authentic leader will see it simply as the failure of the project or approach and their sense of self will remain untouched. This is a marked change. The dysfunctional ego would have seen things quite differently and translated the simple failure of a project into their personal failing and would have been deeply affected emotionally.

The leadership benefits as we move into authentic leadership are tangible. The authentic leader is able to remain clear headed and in emotional equilibrium even in stressful and testing situations, and like the *Conscious Leader* they are capable of bringing calm to chaos and clarity to confusion.

Another important shift has also taken place. If you listen to an authentic leader talking you will notice they use different language to those at the dysfunctional and functional stages. Instead of constant references to 'I', 'me' and 'mine' and to 'making' and 'getting' people to do things, the authentic leader is beginning to talk in terms of 'we', 'our' and how to 'enable' people to achieve. This significant shift in language and mindset is a direct and natural consequence of beginning to transcend the ego.

When we are rooted in ego, we see the world as existing to serve us. When we transcend ego, we spontaneously see our role as one of service to the world. This shift in language and attitude shows we are beginning to set ego aside and lead from a higher level of consciousness. It brings release and focus to the leader, but the benefits to those they lead are even more significant.

Those fortune enough to be led by a leader at the *authentic* level feel valued, enabled and supported. They are able to develop, use their creativity and understand and feel committed to their leader's vision, not least because it includes and values them and what they contribute. Authentic leaders are concerned not with themselves but have a clear understanding of, and commitment to, the greater good because as we transcend ego our role becomes that of serving those who follow us.

The concept of Servant Leader

The idea of servant leadership is not new in itself; it has, in fact, been around for millennia. In the 1970s, Robert Greenleaf embodied the notion of service into a model of servant leadership. My experience in working with those executives who are prepared to commit to the entire leadership journey is that, as they become increasingly ego-less in their leading, their desire to serve others spontaneously arises; the impulse to serve being a natural consequence of setting the ego aside. For this reason, I do not recommend *trying* to serve; instead simply seek to do so when the impulse arises. Above everything else, our first and main aim remains to become aware of, and to gently set aside, the ego.

However, when the impulse to serve does arise, a framework for understanding the mechanics, or the key elements to the process of servant leadership, is useful. To this end, *Conscious Leadership* incorporates the ideas behind servant leadership in order to enable the leader to achieve the final refinements in their leadership evolution.

Rooted in the position of authentic leadership, the *Conscious Leadership* model maintains that there are two foundation practices which underpin the ability to serve others. The first is 'intent' or 'will' and the second is 'agape love' or, in other words, the unconditional regard for another person's humanity. These foundations are key to achieving *Conscious Leadership* and they are further explored and incorporated into the '*Six Practices of a Conscious Leader*', examined fully in the next section.

For now we need only know that cultivating these ways of being creates a position of service in which a leader sacrifices willingly his or her personal agendas and glory for the sake of the greater good. The Greenleaf Model sets out the outcome of this position: a leader's ability to engender deep trust and respect and the conferring of authority upon them. It is important to understand the difference between, 'power' and 'authority' in this context; the first is something seized by the ego-full leader whereas the second is given to the leader by their followers.

Needless to say that 'authority' is where real power lies. When a leader occupies this space, they have achieved deep trust, loyalty and buy-in from those they lead. This is the basis of leadership for the *Conscious Leader*. So, if you have reached the *authentic leadership* level, now is the time to focus on cultivating the final transition to *Conscious Leadership*.

Achieving Authentic Leadership

There is no separate process to be gone through to move from a functional ego state to authentic leadership. Rather, it is about a deeper level of development. The Three Pillars of Confidence are still key and underpin every step of the journey towards *Conscious Leadership*. What happens as we move through the stages is that we develop and embed these pillars more and more fundamentally.

As our work on self worth, self trust and self acceptance initially helps us move from a dysfunctional to functional ego state, here, as they are further developed and applied in our day to day interactions and leadership of others, they help us begin to transcend ego altogether. That is the shift. It is a tipping point and you will recognise it when it happens.

We are now on the verge of the highest level of leadership development; as our sense of service and purpose deepens, humility spontaneously emerges as the final quality that tips us into *Conscious Leadership* territory.

Recognising the Authentic Leader:

As the move from functional ego to authentic leader is truly transformative, representing a shift from being predominantly ego-full to becoming predominantly ego-less, we see real changes in attitudes, outlooks and behaviours. Authentic leaders:

- Are profoundly relaxed and comfortable in their own skin, even under considerable pressure
- Can deal swiftly and easily with difficult people and situations, preserving a sense of fairness and integrity throughout
- Are able to hold apparently conflicting or paradoxical ideas and issues, bringing calm to chaos and clarity to confusion

- Have a strong sense of self which embraces openly both individual strengths and weaknesses and which remains robust and intact under pressure
- Talk more often of, 'we', 'our' and 'enabling' others to achieve rather than focusing on what others can do for them
- Are much more concerned about meeting the needs of others to enable the common goal than pursuing their own agenda or personal glory

Towards Conscious Leadership

When we have established ourselves completely as authentic leaders, focused on meeting the needs of others rather than on ourselves, we are ready to begin the final stage of our journey and move towards *Conscious Leadership*. Now we work to transcend ego entirely and lead from beyond a limited sense of self.

Whilst our journey is still underpinned by continuing to work with the Three Pillars of Confidence, at this more advanced level we are ready to engage in the six practices that refine and nurture *Conscious Leadership*, allowing the ego to be ever more easily and gently set aside.

The six practices of the Conscious Leader

The practices of the *Conscious Leader* require lifelong commitment. They are not something achieved and then forgotten, but require constant refinement and development. However, the rewards for working on these six practices will be profound, benefiting those you lead and the organisations for which you work, as well as moving your own sense of self beyond the restrictions and confinement associated with ego.

Practice One - Cultivating awareness

This is the foundation stone of all the practices of a *Conscious Leader*. Through expanding our awareness we see how our ego manifests itself and limits us. We are also able to understand and prioritise both our own needs and those of others and we are able to know and understand our vision and how to deploy our skills.

To fully cultivate awareness, we must first cultivate stillness. Stillness facilitates true awareness, creating the space for a real depth of understanding. Without stillness we are too readily lost in a maelstrom of thoughts, and prone to follow familiar, well worn but often ultimately unproductive thought patterns and actions. This serves to drown out our intuition and cloud our ability to perceive and understand the unspoken needs or agendas of others and so leaves us unable to respond adeptly or completely.

> *When you are not doing anything the energy moves towards the centre, it settles down towards the centre. When you are doing something the energy moves out. Doing is a way of moving out. Non-doing is a way of moving in.*
> Osho

Creating stillness is a huge challenge. We live in a world full of stimuli, of instant gratification, and we are incessantly bombarded by multiple demands on our time and resources.

True peace and quiet is a rare commodity to most of us, and for those of us in senior leadership positions it is a particularly scarce resource. Yet, no matter how busy we are, or how many conflicting priorities or people are vying for our attention at any one time, we do have a choice.

The fact is busyness is an easy state to fall into and a difficult one to escape. This is not simply because of the pace and demands of modern leadership and life, it is because for many of us busyness has become a means of distracting ourselves from issues we would rather not explore. A few minutes of silence can seem threatening, and if this is the case for you, start by asking yourself what it is you are avoiding or possibly even fearful about.

If you are committed to becoming the best leader you can be, you must be committed to creating the time and space for stillness. There are always a hundred reasons why it is hard to make the time: deadlines to meet, children to spend time with, too little spare time; the potential list is endless. Stillness, therefore, has to be an active choice and the fact is to make real strides forward and become a truly transformational leader you must make the time for stillness.

> *Laziness consists of cramming our lives with compulsive activity*
> *so that there is no time at all to confront the real issues*
> Sogyal Rinpoche

There is no better practice for cultivating stillness than through meditation. Meditation is the science and technology of awareness, and the most profound tool for its cultivation; the art of non-doing which creates stillness. As we cultivate the state of non-doing we become centred and totally present, living in the present moment. It is only from achieving this presence - the centred state in which we are totally and utterly living only in the moment - we can really become totally aware, intuitive and, free from attachment, cultivate our 'inner witness'.

This sense of stillness produced by meditation is an integral part of *Conscious Leadership* and an essential practice for the *Conscious Leader*. Without a stillness practice efforts to expand our level of consciousness and so help ourselves move beyond ego will be hampered. Stillness and mindfulness bring their own psychological benefits, often helping those who pursue such practices feel calmer, more satisfied, have a better outlook and to sleep better.

> *If we really knew how unhappy it was making this whole planet that we all try to avoid pain and seek pleasure - how that was making us so miserable and cutting us from our basic heart and basic intelligence - then we would practice meditation as if our hair was on fire . . . there wouldn't be any question of thinking we had a lot of time and that we could do this later.*
>
> Pema Chondron

There are many different forms of meditation and there is almost certainly an approach that will suit you. Working with a teacher or as part of a meditation class will help you establish your own, sound practice and will also help you avoid the many misconceptions that abound and easily frustrate the inexperienced practitioner. However, here is a simple meditation practice that is completely accessible to anyone, whether they have meditated before or they are a complete beginner.

Simple Meditation Exercise

- *In peaceful surroundings and a comfortable position, take a minute to relax your mind and body. Close your eyes and mouth, breathing normally through your nose. Take a few deep breaths to help you relax*
- *Now turn your attention inwards, away from outside thoughts and influences and towards stillness, focusing on your breathing all the time. Become aware of your breath, as you inhale and as you exhale, and then begin to slowly breathe into your abdomen*
- *Simply be, focussing on your breathing to help you stay in purely mindful, present state. Turn your attention inward and find the silent stillness of your mind. Feel the silence and rest in it. If you become distracted by thoughts, simply turn your focus back to your breathing before retuning back to the silence*

Ideally aim to meditate for twenty minutes in the mornings and evenings, but if this is not practical or possible to start with, just do as much as you can. Five minutes is much better than not doing it at all.

Do not worry if you do find yourself thinking a lot to start with; this is perfectly normal. Over time, quietening your mind and connecting with stillness will become much easier; it just takes practice.

Practice Two - Cultivating acceptance

The second key practice of the *Conscious Leader* is that of surrender and acceptance. This will arise naturally as a direct result of cultivating the awareness borne of stillness, but it still takes time to master the practice of acceptance. In many ways, it is a lifetime's work and a whole new way of being. However, there is no need to feel overwhelmed or disheartened because although mastery may take many years, considerable benefits can be achieved relatively quickly.

As we cultivate awareness and mindfulness through our stillness practice, we develop a new and deepening connection to the 'witnessing observer' (also defined as pure awareness or consciousness itself) within us and learn to become increasingly present and in the 'now'. As we become present, we become more and more aware of our conditioned, reactionary behaviour patterns and how these are triggered by various external stimuli. As we see and understand these reactions more clearly we eventually come to a point where we begin to notice how much we struggle with what simply 'is', or our current reality. This struggle is that of ego; and it is, of course, the ego that is at war with reality.

Our ego contains the imprint of all our attachments: what we like and what we dislike, what we seek and what we avoid, and what we accept and what we reject. At the root of the issue is whether what we are experiencing makes us feel more or less safe. If events increase our feelings of safety, then we will crave more; if what happens undermines our sense of security, then we aim to reject or avoid it.

Cultivating acceptance is not about being passive, but it is about cultivating a sense of release and relaxation which allows for calm clarity and dealing with situations more effectively. As we are all too aware, leadership is full of testing and difficult situations. The practice here helps us to become aware of our 'like/don't like' minds and to lay the foundations for cultivating acceptance.

Exercises for cultivating acceptance

The following exercises will help you begin to cultivate a greater sense of acceptance in the light of the shifting sands on which we all stand on a daily basis.

Exercise One - Knowing our minds

This part of awareness practice is about becoming super aware of the 'like/don't like mind'. Again, we must apply the practice of mindfulness to become cognizant of these patterns. Once you begin to look at and register these reactions, you will be surprised just how many times a day we judge what is happening to us, and indeed to others, as being good or bad, right or wrong, acceptable or unacceptable. We use our awareness of our language and our emotions as clues to when the 'like/don't like mind' has been triggered, and this can be as simple and literal as listening to ourselves say "I don't like that" or "I like that", or it might be much more subtle. Subtle indicators might include a slight feeling of anxiety, a perfect reason that we invent to avoid somebody or something or particularly cunningly, an act of kindness or false humility, which hides the fear of rejection or praise.

Observe the language of your mind and the emotions you experience and key into what you crave more of and what you try to avoid or turn away from. Notice how these patterns impact your equanimity.

Exercise Two—Establishing calm

The 'breathing in' exercise we have already used can be used again to help us establish a sense of calm.

As before, simply identify the negative emotions you would like to replace with a sense of calm and then start to breathe in hot, dark heaviness and exhale a cool, bright and light sense of freshness. Breathe in through every pore of your body, and radiate outwards through every pore. Once you feel totally synchronised with your breathing, begin to work on your particular issue or emotion, replacing the negative emotion with a profound sense of acceptance that all is as it should be.

Exercise Three - Simple reflections

It can also be very helpful to reflect on how absurd, egotistical and ultimately unrealistic it is to expect everything to go our way. Alternatively, or additionally, simply ask yourself: 'If I trusted all is well, how would I respond now?'

Becoming aware of the tricks and conceits of ego is the first important step towards freedom. Once we become aware of our conditioned patterns we need to move forwards. Sometimes it is enough to just shine a light on the problem for it to lose the intensity of its grip on us. Sometimes it involves considerably more effort.

We have two choices when it comes to making a change. We can delve deeply into the root cause of the behaviour, or, in other words, dig down deeply and understand the nature of the conditioned beliefs that limit us. This can be a tricky process and undoubtedly each of us will have many blind spots when it comes to understanding the real issue at hand and, for this reason, I would again suggest working with a professional coach if you choose to go down this route.

There is also another and much simpler, more direct approach. However, for this to be effective you will need to truly understand and accept the false nature of the ego and in so doing to fully understand and accept that our true nature is one defined by limitless potential. If you are able to grasp this concept and understand the ego is no more than a false self, and in essence just the sum total of all the baggage we have been given by others, then the practice of moving beyond it becomes quite straightforward.

Further exercises for cultivating acceptance

Exercise One - Objectifying the ego

When you become aware you are thinking, feeling or acting from the ego, simply label it for what it is and set it aside rather than becoming drawn into the drama. Our natural tendency will be to become involved in the drama, become aware of a thought or feeling and then immediately invest in it, giving it time and attention and allowing it to snowball. This is a typical ego trait.

We are also capable, however, of filtering out extraneous information or noise in our day to day lives and this is what we must do now. We can choose to pay attention to the ego, listen and become involved in the same old dialogue and patterns of behaviour, or, knowing the whole concept of ego is fundamentally flawed, we can choose to acknowledge but ignore it.

If ego rears its head, acknowledge its presence, label it as a false self and then put it to one side and move beyond it. Once you recognise ego at work, it can be helpful to give it a face of some kind; I see it as a grumpy man stomping up and down with red cheeks and blowing hot air, and this works very well for me. Once you have acknowledged the ego's presence, use a verbal anchor to move beyond it. This might be as simple as saying to yourself: "Ah, I understand this is ego talking." You may choose to follow this up with a question such as: "If I was acting from an ego-less place, what would I do, say and think?" These verbal anchors help define new choices and new ways of being which are much more in alignment with higher intentions.

Exercise Two - Two minutes of stillness

When you recognise your ego at work, simply take some time out. Using a meditation practice that suits you, create two minutes of stillness. Simple as this may sound, it is a very powerful method for stopping ego in its tracks.

The witnessing observer will never shout loudly and announce it's presence above the 'noise' that permeates our life; but if we are able to turn the volume down and listen, we will begin to hear and be invisibly guided by its wisdom. When we are able to access the witnessing observer, our decision-making gradually improves and we are able to remain in a greater state of equanimity in response to external events. Our creativity and intuitive capacities are heightened and our actions align more spontaneously with our highest intentions. These are the behaviours and responses of the *Conscious Leader*.

Practice Three - Cultivating equanimity

The third practice of a *Conscious Leader* emerges naturally from the second and is about how we respond to external events. At work, in particular, we are driven at least in part by other people's agendas and need to be able to respond effectively to events, many of which are beyond our own direct control. Our ability to respond appropriately is determined by our equanimity.

Today's leaders face incessant demands to operate at peak performance levels in the face of a relentless high volume load. Many of us are working flat out to meet the demands placed upon us at work. The pace of life has accelerated in recent years, and every day we are bombarded with more and more information and greater stimulation than earlier generations faced in a lifetime. Unsurprisingly, the number of executives suffering from stress, anxiety, insomnia and chronic health problems is on the rise and this is having a significant impact on businesses, particularly when senior leaders are affected.

All of us have experienced stress at some point in our lives, it is a global phenomenon. Chronic stress, which is now rife at the senior executive level, has a far reaching physiological and psychological impact on individuals and is known to be the seed of many of today's most common life-threatening illnesses. In the longer term, stress is a known contributor to high blood pressure, heart disease and cancer; and the more immediate effects include chronic burnout, anxiety and insomnia. These effects have a significant impact in the workplace, contributing to impaired decision-making, absenteeism and lack of engagement.

Yet despite creating working environments in which stress is endemic and putting our leaders under considerable and daily pressure we still look to them to bring calm to chaos and clarity to confusion and expect high levels of personal resilience. The fact is, we cannot establish calm and clarity if we are experiencing chronic stress or we are still in thrall to our reactionary, ego based patterns of behaviour.

If we understand that stress is a physiological and psychological effect that occurs when we either do not get what we want or we get what we do not want, we begin to see a clear connection with ego. The ego, as we know, is rooted in fear, and if something happens that stops or blocks us from doing what we want or having what we wish for, the ego reacts immediately. Our conditioning, beliefs and attachments determine our exact response, but respond we will; and the emotions we experience will be familiar ones such as anger, fear, panic or sadness. Once these emotions are triggered, then our tendency will be to become lost in our own drama. Our ability to see clearly and remain objective is diminished, and if this scenario is repeated over time, we begin to experience chronic stress.

To create the platform for a more measured and objective response, we re-establish balance and equanimity and meditation is again a very powerful tool. As we have seen, meditation allows us to experience inner calm and deep relaxation and on a physiological level, it is a powerful antidote to stress. The practice of meditation also brings increasing clarity and the understanding that we are neither our thoughts nor our emotions. As we meditate, we become aware that there appears to be somebody witnessing our thoughts and emotions. This witnessing observer, a term used by Buddhists, is consciousness itself. You may also see it as your soul or spirit.

Meditation is a mechanism that helps us unhook from the stories we tell ourselves. In the silence of meditation, we come to realise that no matter what thoughts pass through our minds, or what emotions ripple through, or perhaps even grip, our body, the witnessing observer remains gently detached and is always completely untouched by the drama that our mind is creating or the story it is telling. It is a place of infinite calm and safety and when we learn to connect with this place in meditation repeatedly, the experience spills over into our daily lives and we find we have continued access to, and develop a relationship with, this essence.

It can also be very useful, once you have identified and set aside the ego-full behaviours and thoughts, to immediately fill the vacuum with reaffirming our purpose. This is particularly helpful when ego patterns have been holding us back from taking risks, living our dreams and fulfilling our potential. Creating purpose is one of the most powerful catalysts for helping us move forwards when we feel blocked, anxious or afraid and it is an area we will now explore more fully.

Practice Four - The power of purpose

> *There are two great days in a person's life - the day they were born and the day they discovered why*
> S A Sreedharen

Understanding the power of purpose is particularly critical in leadership as it is a sense of purpose that most engages those who follow us; but the fact is we cannot expect others to follow us if we do not ourselves have a clear idea of who we are and where we are heading. Understanding our life's purpose must, therefore, be a priority.

Uncovering the purpose, or the 'why', in our lives is given very little attention today, particularly in proportion to its fundamental importance in establishing our sense of fulfilment and happiness. It is my belief that every one of us has a unique gift, unique talents and unique perspectives that we are meant to contribute to the world. When we fully express this purpose we take part in an extraordinary act of creation which gives us a profound sense of fulfilment.

Unsurprisingly, our sense of purpose emanates from our highest possible sense of self. For this reason, our knowledge of our purpose, let alone our active pursuit and engagement it in it, can be immensely threatening to ego. Following the path of our purpose is certainly the most rewarding and, ultimately, the most sustaining path open to us, even if it is not always the easiest or smoothest path. It can require great things of us and very often asks that we step out of the comfort zone created and guarded fiercely by our ego. It asks us to step forward and lay ourselves open to the judgment, criticism and opprobrium of others.

Of course, it is wryly amusing to note that those people busy criticising, judging and disapproving of our higher purpose are, in fact, most often in the grip of their own egos, determined to keep them in the apparent, but ultimately limiting, safety of their own comfort zones. It is very useful, when subject to the judgements of others, to bear in mind the fact that those judgments are almost certainly a reflection of their own ego patterns rather than a valid comment on any action of yours.

Cultivating a deep familiarity with our own personal purpose gives us deep roots, moving us beyond the judgments of other people's egos and silencing our own. The ability to remain connected to this purpose provides a powerful invisible force; an indispensable ally in helping us move beyond our ego and take positive and purposeful action. So when ego rises up and threatens to take hold of us, reconnecting deeply with our purpose provides a positive energy that balances the negative and constraining forces of the ego's limiting patterns.

Finding our purpose

Connecting with, and establishing true clarity about, our unique purpose requires commitment. It can be a daunting and seemingly complex task and for most of us it will feel rather like mining for precious jewels. We must dig deep and persevere, but if we do, we will be rewarded with a seed of truth that lies at the heart of us and our real, highest mission in life. Often, we will start by finding a 'sense' of our purpose, and we will have to live with this seemingly vague notion for some time. This can seem frustrating but, if this is what you experience, then it will be a necessary phase. It is rather like cutting a flawless diamond from rock: we know the diamond lies within, and yet in this raw state we cannot fully see its full truth and beauty. It then becomes our task to begin to cut away the rock and polish the surface until the ultimate truth of our purpose is revealed.

However, very often I suspect we are closer to understanding our purpose than we realise. The whisper of our intuition, our passions and what we long to do constantly give us clues and signposts as to our true direction of travel. It is just that, time and time again, the ego rises up to sabotage or prevent our understanding of our own truth. The ego shouts much louder than the whispering of our soul and paralyzed by fear and anxiety, the ego keeps us in our own comfort zone.

For most people, a myriad of perfect reasons gives us an entirely plausible excuse for not pursuing our purpose. The ego will certainly do its utmost to keep you within your, or its, comfort zone. The choice you have as a leader, and as a human being, is whether you choose to listen to it or not; but remember that the ego is a false prophet mesmerizing us with its predictions of doom and gloom. If we do fall into ego's thrall, it leads us to arid, unproductive and unfulfilling territory. It cannot and will not allow us to fulfil our highest purpose and achieve true fulfilment.

It is important to see purpose as a process rather than a goal. Our unique purpose is an ongoing expression of who we really are, and this can take a little thought and understanding in such a goal and results orientated world where we devote so much time and effort to achieving the next win or to ticking the next thing off the list. In many respects, we will have a lifelong apprenticeship to our purpose, and this can fly in the face of all our learning and conditioning about progress, achievement and reward.

We must be open to the fact that our sense of purpose is likely to evolve over time and that it needs fulfilling tomorrow, next year and even at the end of your life just as much as it does today. Purpose itself has no inherent outcome or endpoint, although we may choose to set goals that are in alignment with our purpose as we travel along our own unique leadership path. In this way, our purpose is like an inner compass; always pointing toward our true North no matter which direction we face, yet never with a final destination.

However, we know we are acting in alignment with our purpose because we experience a deep sense of fulfilment and inner contentment even though the journey itself can sometimes be demanding and the ride bumpy. We often feel that we are being more 'real' in the world, and our ability to engage with our purpose often leads us to engage more effectively with others, helping us to inspire them to follow our vision.

Once you have chosen to engage with your purpose, the first step is to commit to listening and acting on your own intuition. You must start to listen for and take that inner voice seriously and give it the attention it deserves. You must also give more of your mental energy to 'dreaming the future' allowing yourself to create a vivid and three-dimensional picture of your future and ideal life, and you must start paying exquisite attention to those activities which bring you joy and fulfilment.

Exercises for establishing a sense of purpose

Both these exercises will begin the process of engaging with yourself in understanding how you are uniquely meant to make a difference as a leader.

Exercise One - Making a vision board

Use words and pictures to create a vision of the future for yourself, including how you would like to make a real impact or difference through your unique purpose. Use drawings and pictures and words taken from magazines or newspapers, or anything else that illuminates your vision. They should be words and pictures that are meaningful to you, igniting your passion and drawing you forwards.

Exercise Two - Visualising life

Imagine yourself at the end of your life and tune into what you would like to look back on and what gives you a sense of accomplishment and contentment. Visualise the life you would like to have led and notice what themes arise. Use these visions and feelings to help identify you true purpose and to help draw you forwards. Ask yourself how you made a difference and why that was satisfying for you.

How do you know when you are on the right track?

When you are working in line with your true purpose and values, you will feel energized by the process and this is a strong sign that you are on the right track. Treat the process as if you were painting a masterpiece, something that requires a deep level of attention and love; and give yourself over totally and completely to becoming the person you were always meant to be.

Warning: Ego at work

Of course, the ego will go into overdrive, and the closer you get to understanding your purpose and breathing life into it, the louder its voice will become and the more vehement its attempt to sabotage your progress. In fact, the more 'perfect reasons', excuses and resistance that you meet, and this can take many forms from excessive busyness to eternal procrastination, then the more you can be sure that you are on the right track. You must become the intrepid warrior and keep going regardless of all the ego's incessant prophecies of doom and apocalyptic and imminent self destruction.

Once you have overcome these attempts of ego to pervert your efforts and thwart your progress, it will usually come up with another and often even more persuasive argument. It usually goes something along the lines of "How could you do this to your family - you are just so selfish." This one stops many of us in our tracks, and is the most common 'perfect reason' why people do not even take the first step towards their real purpose and remain unhappy and unfulfilled. Clearly, sometimes our purpose requires a significant shift in lifestyle and requires considerable planning. This is no reason not to pursue it. There is, in fact, no reason whatsoever for us not to fulfil our real and higher purpose. It all comes down to choice, and that choice is ours.

Practice Five - The role of intent

The final two practices of a *Conscious Leader* relate specifically to how the leader facilitates the highest level of performance in their followers. As we have already mentioned, the ancient concept of servant leadership is embodied in the *Conscious Leadership* model and turns our current paradigm of leadership on its head. Now the leader is no longer served by his followers; the roles are reversed and the leader seeks to understand and fulfil the needs of those they lead.

It is not uncommon for the newly emerging *Conscious Leader*, whose behaviour is increasingly rooted in service, to fear they will lose their edge and forfeit the efficient delivery of the organisation's objectives. It is important not to indulge these fears. The role of the leader remains clear. They must retain their visionary capacity and the ability to translate this into strategy and deliverables. So in order to remain effective, the *Conscious Leader* requires both pristine clarity of vision and intent and the ability to communicate expectations and objectives clearly.

The leader's role is to use their expanded state of awareness to anticipate and interpret the needs of followers; to understand and remove any resistance or obstacles that may stand in the way of the successful delivery of outcomes. It may be that very often followers are not able, or aware enough, to recognise and identify those obstacles. This is where the sophisticated leader needs to use their heightened awareness not only to notice existing needs, but also anticipate them before they arise.

Of all the practices, this is the one most leaders will be familiar with as it is closely aligned with the usual business practice of setting goals and objectives. Most people set goals and therefore have a clear intent, but they fail to communicate this intent effectively or often enough.

Furthermore, it is essential that the *Conscious Leader* is not only clear when setting and communicating objectives, but is also able to hold people to account effectively when they do not deliver.

In my experience, it is this part of the process which is most difficult for leaders who are deeply rooted in ego because they often fear the disintegration of the relationship or rejection. However, as we become more adept at moving beyond our ego, we also become more fluent with the practice of separating the problem from the individual. Drawing upon agape love, a concept we will shortly explore fully, we can create a model for dealing with 'difficult' situations in which we create strong boundaries and clear messages about behaviour and delivery. At the same time the model requires that we maintain both our own integrity and the positive intent of helping the follower to learn and grow; this utterly respects the integrity of the individual with whom we are dealing.

Exercises for establishing intent

The following exercises will assist you in maintaining a clear intent and ensuring delivery within a framework which maintains strong and loyal relationships built on integrity, trust and respect.

Exercise One - The prompt

To understand how clear you are about your sense of purpose and direction, simply ask people to tell you your vision or intent. If they are unable to tell you, you need to communicate your vision more effectively and / or more frequently.

Exercise Two - Making dealing with difficult situations easier

These simple devices can help immensely when approaching difficult or uncomfortable situations:

- *Write down a list of adjectives which describe how you currently feel when you think about 'conflict', such as destructive, uncomfortable, anxiety-provoking, adversarial, etc.*

- *Now reframe 'conflict' to 'collaboration' in your own mind and transform your list of negative adjectives into positive, collaborative ones. Once you have a new list, from now on, memorise it, noticing how different you feel and what new opportunities become available when we see so called 'difficult' conversations as opportunities for learning, growth, collaboration, etc. Always hold this new list of adjectives in your mind when approaching 'difficult' scenarios. The more you embrace and breathe life into them, the more different, effective behaviours will become accessible to you in resolving these types of scenarios.*

- *Before entering any 'difficult' conversation, create an ideal outcome in your head, or the best possible situation given the circumstances. Again use positive, collaborative language about the opportunities this interaction presents to get yourself into a resourceful state before engaging with the problem.*

Exercise Three - Effective ways of dealing with performance issues

When trying to understand poor performance you need to drill down to the root of the matter, not just look at the symptoms. These devices will help you achieve this:

- *Do not start a conversation about performance without a clear understanding of the desired outcome, and do not leave the room until you have achieved a satisfactory level of outcome*
- *Bear in mind you may need a series of conversations to get to the root of the matter, not just one*
- *Use the framework described above to help you create a collaborative opportunity for problem solving.*
- *Remember, it is not just what you say, but how you say it. Hold on to a positive intent about helping an individual develop and enable growth and reflect this in your approach*
- *Do not let things fester because this inevitably results in worsening an already challenging situation. Facing up to the situation and engaging in these conversations will make things better and will get easier as you progress through setting aside the ego*
- *Always have your 'bottom line' of what is acceptable and what is not. One of the most common reasons why poor performance continues in my experience is because a leader does not set clear boundaries and consequences, or is not prepared to follow through if boundaries are transgressed.*

Practice Six - Agape Love

I think most of us would agree that the word 'love' is one that is not commonly associated with leadership, nor is it one we hear bandied around the boardroom. In fact, the prevailing business culture is one in which we have sought to totally exorcise such feelings and, in many ways, actually conceal ourselves. One of my clients summed this up perfectly recently when he revealed he considered himself as having two lives. The first was his business persona which he referred to as Mr. Jones and the second his personal persona, for which he used his first name. Both characters dressed, spoke and even thought completely differently.

This clinical approach to our working environments, in which we have systematically sought to remove heart, soul and passion from the workplace, is the approach in which most of us have been raised. The good news is that things have begun to shift. There is a growing acceptance that more supportive and empathetic working environments produce better results and we hear the term 'authentic leader' more often, a concept which supports us turning up for work as our true and whole selves rather than as a separate persona. Authentic leadership, and its inherent self acceptance and willingness to be vulnerable, is fundamental to achieving *Conscious Leadership* and is an integral part of our journey. It is not, however, our final destination.

Conscious Leadership takes us beyond authentic leadership. As we have already seen, it is the deepening connection with our true self and our real or higher purpose which drives us spontaneously forwards towards the service of others. However, to reach the pinnacle of our leadership potential and truly become the servant leader, there is one final ingredient; that of agape love. Agape love is an essential component in creating the strongest relationships and it is characterised by a deep level of trust and loyalty.

Agape love is, in essence, the selfless love of others. It expects nothing in return and embodies the ideals of service and leadership. It is the genuine holding of another human being in the highest regard based solely on their shared humanity. Agape love is not influenced by titles, material possessions, accents or lifestyle choices; it is simple, non-judgmental and unquestioning and it is made possible only by our moving beyond the inherent restrictions of our own ego.

The expression of agape love requires that we expand our consciousness way beyond the experience and confines of everyday reality. With the dissolving of the ego and our small sense of self, the *Conscious Leader* becomes increasingly aware of the similarities rather than the differences that exist between us. They easily see beyond the accoutrements of the ego and are increasingly concerned with connecting with the human being that lies hidden beneath because at this level of development, there is often a spontaneous unfolding of awareness and understanding of the interconnectedness of life.

This mindset can have a profound effect on how we interact with, behave towards and communicate with our colleagues. The consequence is that others, whether consciously or subconsciously, feel accepted and valued in the most profound way. For the recipient of this type of love, it is enormously powerful and often results in a deep bond of loyalty and respect for the giver. It is in this way, through the fostering of total acceptance that *Conscious Leadership* builds highly effective relationships defined by a robust foundation of trust and mutual respect.

To cultivate this agape love, the practice for a *Conscious Leader* is an active commitment to see beyond behaviour and seek the true nature of other human beings. The simple fact is, most people do not come to work each day to intentionally cause disruption and difficulties, and a powerful practice for the *Conscious Leader* is to continually ask themselves what 'pain' a person is experiencing that is causing them to react in the way they do. More often than not, when we take the time to see the root cause and suffering behind someone's behaviour, we become more able to relate to them and help them find a solution. As leaders, this helps us solve apparently intractable problems.

An exercise in cultivating Agape Love

One of the most powerful techniques for developing agape love is through compassion. When we dissolve boundaries between ourselves and others, we begin to see ourselves as the other person, experiencing the same joys, triumphs and suffering.

In this exercise we repeat the process of the Breathing in Fear exercise we used to help dissipate our own fears and insecurities in the Functional Ego section. This time we expand our consciousness to concentrate on building our compassion for and connection to other people.

Start by identifying the issues or emotions you want to deal with and then rest your mind for a moment or two. Start the exercise by focusing on texture and as you breathe in, feel a hot, dark heaviness; and, as you breathe out, exhale a cool, bright and light sense of freshness. Breathe in through every pore of your body, and radiate outwards through every pore. Continue with this until you feel totally synchronised with your breathing.

Now start work on the issue or emotion you have identified. If this is anger, for example, breathe that in and then breathe out confidence and calm and understanding, or any other emotion or state you would like to replace it with. Again, start by doing this just for yourself and then after a couple of minutes expand it to include others. Begin with people you know well and then gradually expand your scope to include strangers and ultimately all sentient beings experiencing the same issue.

The following provides a snapshot overview of the 'Six Practices', including the key, founding principle behind each one:

Six Practices of *Conscious Leaders*

- **Awareness**—developing a full understanding of ourselves and our egos through stillness
- **Acceptance**—through connecting with our inner 'witnessing observer'
- **Equanimity**—a measured response to external events
- **Purpose**—uncovering and expressing our unique gifts and purpose
- **Intent**—establishing and maintaining clarity of vision and ensuring delivery
- **Agape love**—compassion or the selfless love of others, the foundation of powerful relationships

Stage Four
Conscious Leadership

As the authentic leader develops a deeper sense of awareness and witnessing presence, their consciousness inevitably expands; they become a committed yet, paradoxically, a more unattached observer who does not get sucked into the drama. It is from this expansion that the final phase of evolution occurs and the *Conscious Leader* emerges.

This is the final stage of the *Conscious Leadership* journey, the movement from an ego-full to an ego-less way of being. As the leader arrives at this stage they have developed a deep level of self acceptance. This gives them a compelling presence and yet in a sense this is paradoxical because they now lead from beyond a limited sense of self and become a catalyst for transformation.

Conscious Leaders eschew the limelight and instead focus their attention elsewhere. Unconcerned with their profile, acclaim or the judgments of others, they understand and accept their strengths, their brilliance and their flaws.

Conscious Leadership **and service**

As leaders begin to lead from an expanded state of consciousness, they naturally step into the role of servant leader. From the deep self acceptance they have achieved comes a deep understanding of the humanity of others and we see the emergence of humility, one of the defining characteristics of the *Conscious Leader*. This humility cannot be created, it simply emerges from an absence of ego; ego and humility being mutually exclusive. However, there is real strength in this humility, a strength driven by a clarity of higher purpose and shared intent made possible by the absence of ego.

> *If humility seems to be an outdated concept in a fiercely competitive world, it's because humility is misunderstood, understudied and underused-and, consequently, underestimated. As an indispensable trait of great leadership, humility must make its way past the pulpit of Sunday sermons and into cubicles and boardrooms. Humility should be our first reflex, not our regret once the moment has passed.*
> David Marcum and Steven Smith

Now able to consciously choose to set aside ego totally and finally, *Conscious Leaders* are deeply focused on understanding and serving the needs of others to fulfil a broader and higher purpose. They are also intensely aware of the role and contribution of others to the greater good and to their own position. For this reason they shun the limelight; they are simply acutely aware that much of what is achieved comes through, rather than from, a *Conscious Leader*. There is no need for external acclaim or approval or appreciation. In stark contrast to the dysfunctional leader, the *Conscious Leader* is what we would call internally referenced.

Reaching Conscious Leadership

Unlike the move from functional to authentic leader which is one of transformation, the move from authentic leadership to *Conscious Leadership* is one of transition; a final refinement. The underlying process of change has remained the same: healing ourselves through developing ever deeper and more robust and sustainable levels of self trust, self worth and self acceptance. The result is a profound level of acceptance allowing a leader to lead from beyond a limited sense of self.

For those who reach *Conscious Leadership* level, the rewards come in terms of liberation from ego, from fear and from the need for visible rewards and external referencing. For those they lead and serve, the rewards are much greater.

Recognising the *Conscious Leader*:

Conscious Leaders are rare beings in today's leadership culture. You may not have encountered one yet, but if you have, they will have had a profound impact. They are truly ego-less, and their path is one of genuine service where they put the good of the whole before self aggrandizement. They embody in all they do the ethos of 'we' rather than 'me'. *Conscious Leaders*:

- Display exceptionally high levels of equanimity in trying circumstances
- Rarely seek the limelight; they are instead happy to place the glory at the feet of others
- Have a deep and profound understanding that much of what is attained comes through and not from them
- See relationships are central to success and show an all pervasive sense of the deepest respect for the humanity of those that they work with

- Always put the good of the whole before their own personal agenda
- Are always willing to recognise their vulnerabilities and weaknesses openly and are not perturbed by loss of status or power if this is what is required to serve a higher purpose and meet the broader goals

Part Three

The Road Ahead

The Road Ahead

As an Executive Coach, I have witnessed first hand too many leaders, and indeed organisations, being held back or, in some cases torn apart, by ego-full leadership. They are drained of energy, inspiration, motivation and commitment and this is a disaster both for the individuals concerned and for the businesses they lead. The ripple effect of such dysfunction and stagnation means a whole organisation can be polluted quickly and easily, putting the long term health of the whole business at risk.

A real thirst for change now exists. Some of the world's most notable leaders and commentators are talking about the need for a new way of thinking in leadership and the vast majority of people I work with, and I believe the majority of senior leaders working today, are looking for a different and better way of leadership; one that inspires, engages and truly rewards those we lead and delivers a whole new level of results. *Conscious Leadership* is that alternative.

The benefits to the individual leader and to those they lead and the organisations for which they work are profound. *Conscious Leadership* delivers true personal resilience, clarity of purpose, new levels of creativity and trust. It will give you new levels of fulfilment and a truly liberating fearlessness. In short, it will help you become the leader you have always wanted to be and that those you lead have always wanted.

Achieving *Conscious Leadership* is not an easy task. It takes discipline and real commitment to new practices, and this can feel hard to accept in today's culture of instant gratification where we have all learned to expect immediate results and look constantly to the next quick win. Sustainability, vision, loyalty and engagement require a long term view and long term effort.

The vast majority of people who set out on the journey towards *Conscious Leadership* do so from a predominantly ego-full state. This is not surprising given the state of leadership in Western culture. Usually, there is a strong dysfunctional ego component in their way of leading which I believe, stems from and reflects the wider societal trend of focusing on the importance of the individual and the immediate, rather than the collective and the longer term.

While each person's move towards an ego-less way of leading will be different, a common theme emerges time and time again: the need to heal oneself before the spontaneous capacity to serve others can emerge. To try to present ourselves as serving others if we are not healed ourselves is simply delusional; such service is built on the flimsiest of foundations, is fundamentally incongruous, and will collapse the moment ego feels challenged.

For many of us, that healing and the process of moving towards *Conscious Leadership* will at times feel circular, and we will revisit the various stages of the process a number of times. The *Three Pillars of Confidence* do take time to build but the work we do here is critical. Rest assured that each time we revisit a stage or process, we achieve greater depth and build firmer foundations.

The journey towards *Conscious Leadership* is not an easy one, but there is no doubt that it is important and rewarding. I have seen time and time again how moving beyond ego extends our potential and makes new level of success possible, regardless of the starting point. For those who are committed to becoming the very best leader they can, embracing *Conscious Leadership* will lead to a new, enlightened and fulfilling way of being and I promise you your efforts will be rewarded.

Bibliography

Easwaran, E. '*The Upanishads*'. 1987. Nilgiri Press

Dilts, R. '*New Tools for a World in Transformation*'. Workbook produced by International Teaching Seminars – not published.

Marcum, D. and Smith, S. 'Egonomics: *What Makes Ego our Greatest Asset (or Most Expensive Liability)*'. 2009. Pocket Books

Tolle, E. '*A New Earth: Create a Better Life*'. 2009. Penguin Books

Williams, N. '*Powerful Beyond Measure*'. 2003. Bantam Books

Resources

The following is a collation of some of the people, organisations and books that have inspired me in my own *Conscious Leadership* journey to date; plus a few others that have been personally recommended to me over the years and can provide additional information on many of the subjects raised in this book.

Meditation Training and Information on Mindfulness

http://www.chopra.com/: The Chopra Centre based in California, US delivers training in Primordial Sound Meditation.

http://theartofmeditation.org/about-meditation-teacher-burgs/: A UK based meditation teacher of exceptional quality.

http://www.tm.org/: Transcendental Meditation training with global reach.

http://www.meditationtrust.com/-A charity providing Meditation training and development.

http://www.bemindful.co.uk/-UK campaign for mindfulness.

http://www.bangor.ac.uk/mindfulness/-Mindfulness research and practice-Bangor University.

http://www.osho.com/: Sometimes controversial, but powerful, teachings on the ego from Osho.

Self Mastery with NLP

Several of the practices listed in the Dysfunctional and Functional ego stages are NLP based; a powerful set of tools and techniques for personal growth and development. There are multitudes of courses available which train people to NLP practitioner levels and above. Even though you might not want to practice professionally, attending a course is a powerful adjunct to personal development work. These are two of the best

http://www.nlpu.com/NewDesign/NLPU.html: Based in California, the NLP University is run by Robert Dilts, a pioneer and master at belief change work.

http://www.itsnlp.com/: Run high quality UK based courses on NLP.

Servant Leadership

http://www.greenleaf.org/

Recommended reading

Hunter, J.C. '*The Servant: A Simple Story about the True Essence of Leadership*'. 1998. Prima

Osho. '*Fame, Fortune and Ambition: What is the Real Meaning of Success?*' 2010. St. Martin's Griffin

Ricard, M. '*Happiness: A Guide to Developing Life's Most Important Skill*'. 2007. Atlantic Books

Taylor, S. '*The Fall: The Insanity of the Ego in Human History and the Dawning of a New Era*'. 2005. O-Books

Tolle, E. '*A New Earth: Create a Better Life*'. 2009. Penguin Books

A Conscious Leadership Story:
Nayar, V. '*Employees First, Customers Second: Turning Conventional Management Upside Down*'. 2010. Harvard Business Press.

About the Author

Dr. Sarah A. Morris is Partner & Executive Coach at The Parallax Partnership, a bespoke Executive Coaching, Leadership Development and OD firm. The Parallax Partnership is a partnership of highly trained and fully accredited executive coaches who are experts in the field of behavioural change and leadership development. We deliver remarkable coaching programmes for senior executives as well as innovative OD solutions which include our unique Experiential Metaphor™ portfolio. Companies hire 'The Parallax Partnership' to solve one or more of these problems:

- To actualize leadership potential in their senior executives

- To create High Performing Teams

- To create more effective, engaging, creative and sustainable cultures

If you wish to contact The Parallax Partnership to explore how we might be able to assist you or your organisation break through to a new level of performance, or simply to request a brochure, please contact us at:

Email: info@parallaxuk.com
Tel No: 00 44 (0) 1285 771104